RULES OF THE ROAD EVERYONE CAN UNDERSTAND.

A COPY OF WHICH IS REQUIRED ON BOARD

ALL VESSELS 12 METERS (39.4 FEET)

OR GREATER IN LENGTH.

EXPERT INTERPRETATIONS AND EXPLANATIONS

ARE INCLUDED ON FACING PAGES MAKING THIS

A QUICK REFERENCE AND STUDY GUIDE FOR

YACHTSMEN, SEAMEN, FISHERMEN,

WATCH OFFICERS, WATCH STANDERS

AND ASPIRING COAST LICENSE CANDIDATES.

This volume is lovingly dedicated to Wade, Doug and Linda and to our days that were...when the roads were long and wet and the Rules were very short.

May they be as happy for Joshua, Joey and little Hannah.

GONDER'S

RULES OF THE ROAD

AN EXACT COPY OF THE OFFICIAL VERSION

WITH FACING PAGE COMMENTS

INCLUDING THE NEW 1991 ADDITIONS

AS LEGALLY REQUIRED ABOARD

VESSELS 12 METERS

OR GREATER IN LENGTH

**Especially Designed As
A Coast Guard License
Study Guide**

5th Edition

EDITED BY

BUDD GONDER

Charters West

Publications

CHARTERS WEST P.O. BOX 597 SUMMERLAND, CA. 93067

Library of Congress Cataloging-in-Publication Data

Gonder, Budd

[Rules of The Road.]
Gonder's Rules of The Road : an exact copy of the official version : with facing page comments including the new 1991 additions, as legally required aboard vessels 12 meters or greater in length / edited by Budd Gonder. -- 5th ed.
p. cm.
"Especially designed as a Coast Guard license study guide."
Includes Index

ISBN 0-9613913-7-5 : $12.95
1. Rules of the road at sea. 2. Inland navigation--Law and legislation--United States. I. Title.

VK371.G58 1990
623.88'84--dc20 90-83771
CIP

FOR VIDEO, BOOK AND ACCESSORY ORDERS
PLEASE CONSULT PAGES 223-224

The ability of a new boat owner to navigate his craft within the confines of a harbor is inversely proportionate to the size of his new toy.

This is the fifth edition of the Rules of The Road as published by Charters West. In this edition the International Rules and accompanying comments on facing pages are presented first. The artwork is then presented followed by the Inland Rules and last the respective Annexes for both International and Inland. The Table of Contents was designed for an easy search pattern.

Differences between the two sets of Rules are emphasized in a way that one is not likely to forget them.

Examples of our simplicity is exemplified by both the comments on facing pages adjacent to each Rule and the mid-volume graphics on pages 89-104.

Still, the Rules are the Rules and as such we are in constant fear of being sued by some pharmaceutical company for having found a viable but unlicensed cure for insomnia.

For aspiring licensees seeking a coveted scroll of expertise in the form of a mariner's ticket from the Coast Guard, here is the chance to regress to a kinder age while absorbing pure knowledge. No doubt about it, they will entertain only experts in their exam rooms.

Buy some felt pens and make a coloring book out of pages 90-99. You'll learn something in the process.

TABLE OF CONTENTS

AN INTRODUCTION TO SAVE CONFUSION

Changes in the Inland Rules must be by Congressional Mandate for they are law. The five Inland Annexes are Regulations. The COLREGS are **col**lision **reg**ulations meaning regulations to prevent collisions at sea and since they are international in scope they are treaties. Changes therein must be proclaimed by the President when the Maritime Safety Council entertains changes. And, they have so entertained. International changes can be expected regarding Rules 1, 3, 8, and 10 plus two minor changes in Annexes I and IV.

Conforming changes will occur Inland only with Rules 1 & 8 and later in the Annexes when the respective bureaucratic regimes have attended to their duties. Working with computers takes longer. Ask any salesperson working with a Sears cash register. At press time these expected mandates and proclamations had not been made. However, the changes are integrated into this text and *indicated by italics*. They are discussed under the facing page comments for the edification of the boating public at large and for those cramming for their respective Coast Guard exams.

The International acceptance date for these changes was last scheduled for April 19, 1991. Hopefully, by then, Congress and the White House can rally and enact their responsibilities. Still, readers should stand advised that we are dealing here with a burgeoning bureaucracy generally more interested in their own rules than the more pragmatic ones.

Current status of these changes, both Inland and International, can be had by calling **(202) 267-0357;** at least until the phone traffic at that number encourages someone to change the number.

Budd Gonder
Summerland, CA
November - 1990

The new "proposed" Inland changes were referenced in *The Federal Register* / Vol 55, No. 25 / Tuesday, February 6, 1990 / Rules and Regulations.

INLAND VS. INTERNATIONAL WATERS

The dividing lines between Inland and International Rules in the United States are referred to as "demarcation lines." These lines are prominently noted on large scale harbor charts. In most cases it is plainly marked at or near the harbor entrance running from one obvious light or landmark to another of like kind on the opposite side of the harbor entrance. There are exceptions.

Some waters within the continental boundaries are considered International waters. For example, both the Puget Sound and all Alaskan navigable waters are considered International. A great many outlying waters along the northeastern seaboard of the U.S. are also designated International waters. For any particular area refer to the applicable large scale charts of the vicinities.

DISCLAIMER

This volume, and all prior editions, are **not** to be considered official Rules of The Road. This is an exact copy of the original version and legally should substitute for it any place, any time. This volume was published as a study guide for the acquisition of U.S. Coast Guard licenses to carry passengers for hire and licenses to operate crewed vessels on the high seas. The reader should be aware that the opinions contained herein are for license study purposes **only** and were not written and published as legal advice or advice on the practical operation of any vessel afloat.

METRIC MEASURE	U.S.
1000 Meters (M)	3280.8 feet
500M	1640.4 feet
200M	656.2 feet
150M	492.1 feet
100M	328.1 feet
75M	246.1 feet
60M	196.8 feet
50M	164.0 feet
25M	82.0 feet
20M	65.6 feet
12M	39.4 feet
10M	32.8 feet
8M	26.2 feet
7M	23.0 feet
6M	19.7 feet
5M	16.4 feet

PART A - GENERAL

Rule #1

Application

(a) These rules shall apply to all vessels upon the high seas and in all waters connected therewith navigable by seagoing vessels.

(b) Nothing in these Rules shall interfere with the operation of special rules made by an appropriate authority for roadsteads, harbors, rivers, lakes or inland waterways connected with the high seas and navigable by seagoing vessels. Such special rules shall conform as closely as possible to these Rules.

(c) Nothing in these Rules shall interfere with the operation of any special rules made by the Government of any State with respect to additional station or signal lights or whistle signals for ships of war and vessels proceeding under convoy, or with respect to additional station or signal lights for fishing vessels engaged in fishing as a fleet. These additional station or signal lights or whistle signals shall, so far as possible, be such that they cannot be mistaken for any light or signal authorized elsewhere under these Rules.

(d) Traffic separation schemes may be adopted by the Organization for the purpose of these Rules.

(e) *Whenever the Government concerned shall have determined that a vessel of special construction or purpose cannot comply fully with the provisions of any of these Rules with respect to the number, position, range or arc of visibility of lights or shapes, as well as to the disposition and characteristics of sound-signalling appliances such vessel shall comply with such other provisions in regard to number, position, range or arc of visibility of lights or signalling appliances, as her Government shall have determined to be the closest possible compliance with these Rules in respect to that vessel.*

INTERNATIONAL RULE #1 - COMMENTS

1a) The International Rule #1 states that this Rule applies to the high seas and any connecting navigable waters from any country **unless that country makes its own Inland Rules.** The US is a good example as is Rule #1 itself.

b) On the other hand, some countries have no Inland Rules of their own and therefore the International Rules apply "upriver" in those countries. If they make their own Rules, they should approximate those of the International Convention. It is unfortunate that some of our own do not.

c) Notice here we're talking "additional" lights and shapes and rules. The assumption is that existing International Rules should not be negated by the participating members.

d) This section acknowledges that certain exceptions need to be made as regards the ordinary everyday Rules of The Road when it comes to deep Inland situations. These are referred to in the US as Vessel Traffic Services (VTS) situations and are found most often in the US along the Mississippi and its tributaries. Special rules for passing, crossing, overtaking, etc. See Comments on Inland Rule #1 and read Inland Rule #10. The latter is very short.

e) If a country has craft unable to conform to the Rules regarding lights, dayshapes, arcs of visiblity, etc. then hang in tightly as possible to the internationally accepted norm. Also take note of the italics. These are important. Please read the Introduction on page 11.

GENERAL

RULE #2

Responsibility

(a) Nothing in these Rules shall exonerate any vessel, or the owner, master or crew thereof, from the consequences of any neglect to comply with these Rules or of the neglect of any precaution which may be required by the ordinary practice of seamen, or by the special circumstances of the case.

(b) In construing and complying with these Rules due regard shall be had to all dangers of navigation and collision and to any special circumstances, including the limitations of the vessels involved, which may make a departure from these Rules necessary to avoid immediate danger.

INTERNATIONAL RULE #2 - COMMENTS

2a) A crewman can be held as responsible for error as the captain. A seaman standing wheel watch who makes a wrong turn could be found as guilty as the mate responsible for the watch. In short, no matter what your station on the ship, your mistakes are your responsibility. True, the mate or captain is going to catch it, but so is the responsible crewman. The Rule of Good Seamanship prevails. A handy definition of a "good seaman" is one who can innovate in a tight situation and still come out looking good.

2b) No matter what the Rules say, if there's a problem and collision or some other danger is imminent, never mind the Rules, use some common sense and affect an appropriate safe maneuver.

GENERAL

RULE #3

General Definitions

For the purpose of these Rules, except where the context otherwise requires:

(a) The word "vessel" includes every description of water craft, including nondisplacement craft and seaplanes, used or capable of being used as a means of transportation on water.

(b) The term "power-driven vessel" means any vessel propelled by machinery.

(c) The term "sailing vessel" means any vessel under sail provided that propelling machinery, if fitted, is not being used.

(d) The term "vessel engaged in fishing" means any vessel fishing with nets, lines, trawls or other fishing apparatus which restricts maneuverability, but does not include a vessel fishing with trolling lines or other fishing apparatus which do not restrict maneuverability.

(e) The word "seaplane" includes any aircraft designed to maneuver on the water.

(f) The term "vessel not under command" means a vessel which through some exceptional circumstance is unable to keep out of the way of another vessel.

(g) The term "vessel restricted in her ability to maneuver" means a vessel which from the nature of her work is restricted in her ability to maneuver as required by these Rules and is therefore unable to keep out of the way of another vessel.

(Cont'd)

INTERNATIONAL RULE #3 - COMMENTS

This entire Rule is rather obvious, but several comments are justified.

A "vessel not under command" is one that is essentially adrift. This is very closely related to a vessel aground. Even the signals are almost the same. The night light signal for a vessel not under command is two vertically arranged 360 degree red lights high on the mast. When aground, an anchor light is added to this array.

Vessel engaged in fishing does not include one that has trolling lines aft.

In the International Rules, vessels "constrained by draft" are recognized, but not in Inland waters. To say they are not "recognized" is a bit severe, but essentially they have a signal giving them a special right-of-way when operating in a narrow or shallow channel, fairway, river or whatever. However, this does not give other vessels on inland waters the right to restrict the traffic of larger cargo vessels. See Inland Rule #9 and read it very carefully.

Also note the italics in 3h. If you don't know why these words are in italics, read the introduction on page 11.

RULE #3 (Cont'd)

(g)(i) a vessel engaged in laying, servicing or picking up a navigation mark, submarine cable or pipeline;

(ii) a vessel engaged in dredging, surveying or underwater operations;

(iii) a vessel engaged in replenishment or transferring persons, provisions or cargo while underway;

(iv) a vessel engaged in the launching or recovery of aircraft;

(v) a vessel engaged in mineclearance operations;

(vi) a vessel engaged in a towing operation such as severely restricts the towing vessel and her tow in their ability to deviate from their course.

(h) The term "vessel constrained by her draught" means a power-driven vessel which because of her draught in relation to the available depth *and width of navigable water*, is severely restricted in her ability to deviate from the course she is following.

(i) The word "underway" means that a vessel is not at anchor, or made fast to the shore, or aground.

(j) The words "length" and "breadth" of a vessel mean her length overall and greatest breadth.

(k) Vessels shall be deemed to be in sight of one another only when one can be observed visually from the other.

(l) The term "restricted visibility" means any condition in which visibility is restricted by fog, mist, falling snow, heavy rainstorms, sandstorms, or any other similar causes.

INTERNATIONAL RULE #3 - COMMENTS

Note the definition of "underway" in 3i. It might seem simple here, but it's one to remember when dealing with the other rules and exams related thereto.

Number 3k compared with 3l seems rather obvious. Not so. We will take time to discuss this little quirk in later Comments. Just remember where you read it first.

PART B-STEERING AND SAILING RULES

Section I-Conduct of Vessels in Any Condition of Visibility

RULE #4

Application

Rules in this Section apply in any condition of visibility.

RULE #5

Look-out

Every vessel shall at all times maintain a proper look-out by sight and hearing as well as by all available means appropriate in the prevailing circumstances and conditions so as to make a full appraisal of the situation and of the risk of collision.

INTERNATIONAL RULE #4 - COMMENTS

Another simple sounding one, but note it says, *in any conditions of visibility*. In one form or another all of the Rules either apply to 1) clear visibility, 2) restricted visibility (meaning-among other things- fog) or, 3) *all* conditions of visibility. This oft forgotten subject will be discussed more fully under Rules 11 and 19.

INTERNATIONAL RULE #5 - COMMENTS

The concept of lookout can be misleading until an incident hits the courtroom. "Did you have a lookout posted?"

"Well, yessir, judge. We were all lookouts. Plain clear weather. How were we to know this guy would sail right out of the docks where we couldn't see him coming? I know sailboats have the right-of-way over power, but we couldn't see him, judge."

"Please answer the question. Was anyone on board specifically designated as lookout? Did you tell him or her that he or she was the lookout?"

"Well, no judge, you see we could all see..."

Forget it. You just lost your case.

RULE #6

Safe Speed

Every vessel shall at all times proceed at a safe speed so that she can take proper and effective action to avoid collision and be stopped within a distance appropriate to the prevailing circumstances and conditions.

In determining a safe speed the following factors shall be among those taken into account:

(a) By all vessels;
(i) the state of visibility;
(ii) the traffic including concentrations of fishing vessels or any other vessels;
(iii) the maneuverability of the vessel with special reference to stopping distance and turning ability in the prevailing conditions;
(iv) at night the presence of background light such as from shore lights or from back scatter of her own lights.
(v) the state of wind, sea and current, and the proximity of navigational hazards;
(vi) the draft in relation to the available depth of water;

(b) Additionally, by vessels with operational radar:
(i) the characteristics, efficiency and limitations of the radar equipment;
(ii) any constraints imposed by the radar range scale in use;
(iii) the effect on radar detection of the sea state, weather and other sources of interference;
(iv) the possibility that small vessels, ice and other floating objects may not be detected by radar at an adequate range;
(v) the number, location and movement of vessels detected by radar;
(vi) the more exact assessment of the visibility that may be possible when radar is used to determine the range of vessels or other objects in the vicinity.

INTERNATIONAL RULE #6 - COMMENTS

The Coast Guard has developed a unique way of testing someone regarding precisely what this rule states. All CG test questions are multiple choice and full advantage is taken here.

One such question states: Which of the following situations is NOT RELATED to a Safe Speed according to Rule #6?

Imagine the possibilities. And don't forget the special provisions for radar equipped craft. The Rules state that vessels with operational radar should be using their radar in restricted visibility. See Rule 7b.

‡

RULE #7

Risk of Collision

(a) Every vessel shall use all available means appropriate to the prevailing circumstances and conditions to determine if risk of collision exists. If there is any doubt such risk shall be deemed to exist.

(b) Proper use shall be made of radar equipment if fitted and operational, including long-range scanning to obtain early warning of risk of collision and radar plotting or equivalent systematic observation of detected objects.

(c) Assumptions shall not be made on the basis of scanty information, especially scanty radar information.

(d) In determining if risk of collision exists the following considerations shall be among those taken into account:

(i) such risk shall be deemed to exist if the compass bearing of an approaching vessel does not appreciably change.

(ii) such risk may sometimes exist even when an appreciable bearing change is evident, particularly when approaching a very large vessel or a tow or when approaching a vessel at close range.

INTERNATIONAL RULE #7 - COMMENTS

Again, the basic purpose of the Rules is to prevent collision. Thus, this rule states, if in doubt assume you have a collision situation developing and take early action to avoid same. **If you have operational radar aboard, you must use it.** And no fair going for less than a full appraisal of the developing situation. Know it all and know it now.

7(d)(i) means if the craft off your starboard side is approaching at say a 45 degree angle at 0800 and again at 0815 the relative angle of approach is still 45 degrees, you have a collision course. That goes for any angle forward of your beam-either side. On the other hand, consider a large vessel of 600 feet or a tug with a tow astern of 200 yards. The bearing might be changing, but the very lengths of these vessels make the approach a risky one. Summed up - think ahead.

RULE #8

Action to Avoid Collision

(a) Any action taken to avoid collision shall, if the circumstances of the case admit, be positive, made in ample time and with due regard to the observance of good seamanship.

(b) Any alteration of course and/or speed to avoid collision shall, if the circumstances of the case admit, be large enough to be readily apparent to another vessel observing visually or by radar; a succession of small alterations of course and/or speed should be avoided.

(c) If there is sufficient sea room, alteration of course alone may be the most effective action to avoid a close-quarters situation provided that it is made in good time, is substantial and does not result in another close-quarters situation.

(d) Action taken to avoid collision with another vessel shall be such as to result in passing at a safe distance. The effectiveness of the action shall be carefully checked until the other vessel is finally past and clear.

(e) If necessary to avoid collision or allow more time to assess the situation, a vessel shall slacken her speed or take all way off by stopping or reversing her means of propulsion.

(Cont'd)

INTERNATIONAL RULE #8 - COMMENTS

8a) Either do it or don't do it and give yourself plenty of time. None of this wagging back and forth, on again off again maneuvering which does nothing except confuse everyone around you. Keep it simple, direct and soon.

If possible, make speed and course changes big ones so everyone will have a good idea of what you're up to. And avoid coming close to other vessels. This can make some people very skittish. And anyway, what does it prove? That you're a good pilot? Forget it. Ego has no place out there.

If the other operator is a nut, show-off or green with a me-first thing, stay away from him. If he wants half the ocean, give it to him. Eventually, he'll go away and bother someone else.

PLEASE NOTE: This Rule is one with a new additional paragraph (f)(i), (ii) and (iii). See the next page. If the italics don't ring a bell, please read the Introduction on page 11 again.

RULE #8 (Cont'd)

(f)(i) *A vessel which, by any of these rules, is required not to impede the passage or safe passage of another vessel shall, when required by the circumstances of the case, take early action to allow sufficient sea room for the safe passage of the other vessel.*

(ii) *A vessel required not to impede the passage or safe passage of another vessel is not relieved of this obligation if approaching the other vessel so as to involve the risk of collision and shall, when taking action, have full regard to the action which may be required by the rules of this part.*

(iii) *A vessel the passage of which is not to be impeded remains fully obligated to comply with the rules of this part when the vessels are approaching one another so as to involve risk of collision.*

INTERNATIONAL RULE #8 - COMMENTS

No further comments on this Rule.

RULE #9

Narrow Channels

(a) A vessel proceeding along a course of a narrow channel or fairway shall keep as near to the outer limit of the channel or fairway which lies on her starboard side as is safe and practicable.

(b) A vessel of less than 20 meters in length or a sailing vessel shall not impede the passage of a vessel which can safely navigate only within a narrow channel or fairway.

(c) A vessel engaged in fishing shall not impede the passage of any other vessel navigating within a narrow channel or fairway.

(d) A vessel shall not cross a narrow channel or fairway if such crossing impedes the passage of a vessel which can safely navigate only within such channel or fairway. The latter vessel may use the sound signal prescribed in **Rule 34 (d)** if in doubt as to the intention of the crossing vessel.

(e)(i) In a narrow channel or fairway when overtaking can take place only if the vessel to be overtaken has to take action to permit safe passing, the vessel intending to overtake shall indicate her intention by sounding the appropriate signal prescribed in **Rule 34 (c)(i).** The vessel to be overtaken shall, if in agreement, sound the appropriate signal prescribed in Rule **34 c(ii)** and take steps to permit safe passing. If in doubt she may sound the signals prescribed in **Rule 34 (d).**

(e)(ii) This Rule does not relieve the overtaking vessel of her obligation under **Rule 13.**

(f) A vessel nearing a bend or an area of a narrow channel or fairway where other vessels may be obscured by an intervening obstruction shall navigate with particular alertness and caution and shall sound the appropriate signal prescribed in **Rule 34(e).**

(g) Any vessel shall, if the circumstances of the case admit, avoid anchoring in a narrow channel.

INTERNATIONAL RULE #9 - COMMENTS

9a) The term "Narrow Channels" whenever rendered in the Rules should make the fuzzies on the back of your neck stand up. Not only does the International differ from the Inland, but also the signals are different. See Rule 34c and while you're at it, notice the big difference between International and Inland. And remember to stay on the right side of the channel.

9b) Always remember that part about vessels less than 20 meters keeping out of the way of any craft making passage in the channel. Also, any vessel crossing an designated navigable path is definitely the give-way craft, (9d). And note that anyone using the channel even remotely suspecting a problem with a crossing vessel or one, say fishing, in the channel, **may** sound the danger signal, (9d). In the Inland Rule 9(d) it says the danger signal **shall be** sounded. Big difference and a great question for Rules exam. Stop a moment and refer to Inland Comment for Rule 9 and get it straight.

Don't anchor or fish in narrow channels. One would suppose that a narrow channel is termed such relative to the size of the traffic inhabiting it. Basically, you are not supposed to impede traffic which can navigate only within the confines of the designated channel. **Check your chart** for channels marked by buoys or that magenta colored space marking off-shore traffic lanes. Let the big guys go by. If a craft is off the starboard bow in a crossing situation don't assume a 600 foot cargo carrier has to reverse engines while some local crosses the traffic lane in a small boat. Also, not everyone reads the Rules of The Road, like you, and knows this. When getting underway always remember Rule 2b.

RULE #10

Traffic Separation Schemes

(a) This rule applies to traffic separation schemes adopted by the Organization *and does not relieve any vessel of her obligation under any other rules.*

(b) A vessel using a traffic separation scheme shall:
(i) proceed in the appropriate traffic lane in the general direction of traffic flow for that lane;
(ii) so far as practicable keep clear of a traffic separation line or separation zone;
(iii) normally join or leave a traffic lane at the termination of the lane, but when joining or leaving from either side shall do so at as small an angle to the general direction of traffic flow as practicable.

(c) A vessel shall so far as practicable avoid crossing traffic lanes, but if obliged to do so shall cross *on a heading* as nearly as practicable at right angles to the general direction of traffic flow.

(d) Inshore traffic zones shall not normally be used by through traffic which can safely use the appropriate traffic lane within the adjacent traffic separation scheme. However, vessels of less than 20 meters in length and sailing vessels may under all circumstances use inshore traffic zones.

(i) A vessel shall not use an inshore traffic zone when she can safely use the appropriate traffic lane within the adjacent traffic separation scheme. However, vessels of less than 20 meters in length, sailing vessels and vessels engaged in fishing may use the inshore traffic zone.

(ii) Notwithstanding subparagraph (d)(i), a vessel may use an inshore traffic zone when en route to or from a port, offshore installation or structure, pilot station or any other place situated within the inshore traffic zone, or to avoid immediate danger.

(Cont'd)

INTERNATIONAL RULE #10 - COMMENTS

Another Rule with italics. Again, the meaning of these italics is most important. They appear in Rules 1, 3, 8, & 10 and two Annexes. If you have not done so, please read the Introduction on page 11.

Basically, the International Rules recognize two types of traffic lanes. Inshore and those farther to sea used by through traffic. This Rule is to encourage small local craft (particularly those less than 20 meters in length) to use the Inshore Traffic Zones and avoid the large separation zones and traffic lanes offshore. It's okay to *cross* these lanes in a small craft of say less than 100 tons, but it is not wise to join one. In one of these lanes you would find yourself in there travelling side-by-side with the massive cargo vessels.

Vessels entering traffic lanes should do so carefully and at a narrow angle. Don't dash into the middle and hang a quick right or left to join the traffic. Handle it like a freeway on ramp.

On the other hand, when crossing traffic lanes, do so quickly and at a right angle.

Do not anchor near the termination of a traffic zone. You might get run over.

Those soon to challenge the **Coast Guard Rules of The Road module** would do well to take special note of Rule 10(k) and (1)

At this writing the editor admits to ignorance of any so-called "In-shore" traffic zones in the US. True, there may be some.

RULE #10 (Con't)

(e) A vessel other than a crossing vessel or a vessel joining or leaving a lane shall not normally enter a separation zone or cross a separation line except:

- **(i)** in cases of emergency to avoid immediate danger;
- **(ii)** to engage in fishing within a separation zone.

(f) A vessel navigating in areas near the terminations of traffic separation schemes shall do so with particular caution.

(g) A vessel shall so far as practicable avoid anchoring in a traffic separation scheme or in areas near its terminations.

(h) A vessel not using a traffic separation scheme shall avoid it by as wide a margin as is practicable.

(i) A vessel engaged in fishing shall not impede the passage of any vessel following a traffic lane.

(j) A vessel of less than 20 meters in length or a sailing vessel shall not impede the safe passage of a power-driven vessel following a traffic lane.

(k) A vessel restricted in her ability to maneuver when engaged in an operation for the maintenance of safety of navigation in a traffic separation scheme is exempted from complying with this Rule to the extent necessary to carry out the operation.

(l) A vessel restricted in her ability to maneuver when engaged in an operation for the laying, servicing or picking up of a submarine cable, within a traffic separation scheme, is exempted from complying with this Rule to the extent necessary to carry out the operation.

INTERNATIONAL RULE #10 - COMMENTS

Many Rules of The Road module tests of late have been employing a question directed to Rule 10(1), (the last one at the bottom of this page). Candidates would be wise to read carefully and understand this exception to the Rule.

Section II - Conduct of Vessels in Sight of One Another

RULE #11

Application

Rules in this section apply to vessels in sight of one another.

RULE #12

Sailing Vessels.

(a) When two sailing vessels are approaching one another, so as to involve risk of collision, one of them shall keep out of the way of the other as follows:

(i) when each has the wind on a different side, the vessel which has the wind on the port side shall keep out of the way of the other;

(ii) when both have the wind on the same side, the vessel which is to windward shall keep out of the way of the vessel which is to leeward;

(iii) if a vessel with the wind on the port side sees a vessel to windward and cannot determine with certainty whether the other vessel has the wind on the port or on the starboard side, she shall keep out of the way of the other.

(b) For the purposes of this Rule the windward side shall be deemed to be the side opposite to that on which the mainsail is carried or, in the case of a square-rigged vessel, the side opposite to that on which the largest fore-and-aft sail is carried.

INTERNATIONAL RULE #11 - COMMENTS

While the title to Section II might slip by even the most critical eye, consider it carefully. These rules apply **when vessels are within sight of each other.** So, what's the implication? When the fog comes in, when snow makes things impossible to see, when the locusts swarm - these rules do not apply. There will then be an entirely new set of rules. Special maneuvering rules, special rules for signaling, special rules for rights-of-way, etc.

Keep this in mind.

INTERNATIONAL RULE #12 - COMMENTS

A vessel which has the right-of-way is called the "stand-on" craft. A vessel which must give way to the other craft because she does not have the right-of-way is called the "give-way" craft.

12) The rules for sailboats are simple and there are only three:

The sailboat on the starboard tack has the right-of-way.

If both are on a starboard tack, the sailboat to the lee has the right-of-way.

If you can't tell which tack the other sailboat is on when it is to windward, assume it has the right-of-way.

A sailing vessel's tack is defined as that side OPPOSITE over which the **main**boom extends. Try sketching some quick diagrams so you have this straight in case you're not a sailor. All license candidates must know **all** the rules.

RULE #13

Overtaking

(a) Notwithstanding anything contained in the Rules of Part B, Sections I and II of this Section any vessel overtaking any other shall keep out of the way of the vessel being overtaken.

(b) A vessel shall be deemed to be overtaking when coming up with another vessel from a direction more than 22.5 degrees abaft her beam, that is, in such a position with reference to the vessel she is overtaking, that at night she would be able to see only the sternlight of that vessel but neither of her sidelights.

(c) When a vessel is in any doubt as to whether she is overtaking another, she shall assume that this is the case and act accordingly.

(d) Any subsequent alteration of the bearing between the two vessels shall not make the overtaking vessel a crossing vessel within the meaning of these Rules or relieve her of the duty of keeping clear of the overtaken vessel until she is finally past and clear.

RULE #14

Head-On Situations

(a) When two power-driven vessels are meeting on reciprocal or nearly reciprocal courses so as to involve risk of collision each shall alter her course to starboard so that each shall pass on the portside of the other.

(b) Such a situation shall be deemed to exist when a vessel sees the other ahead or nearly ahead and by night she could see the masthead lights of the other in a line or nearly in a line and/or both sidelights and by day she observes the corresponding aspect of the other vessel.

(c) When a vessel is in any doubt as to whether such a situation exists she shall assume that it does exist and act accordingly.

INTERNATIONAL RULE #13 - COMMENTS

13a-b) An excellent definition of overtaking. Basically, IF you cannot see either sidelight, red or green, then you are approaching from behind and the vessel ahead has the right of way. Technically, the only light you will see is the sternlight. This also means it doesn't matter from which side you might be attempting to pass! While overtaking, stay out of the way of the vessel ahead. Recall that sidelights shine from dead ahead to 22.5 degrees abaft the beam. Anyone aft of 22.5 degrees abaft the beam is deemed to be the give-way craft. Interesting: You can see a sidelight or a sternlight, but not both.

13c) What about daytime when sidelights are not normally lighted? This rule says that if in doubt, assume you are the give-way craft.

13d) Once this maneuver is undertaken it is final. No change of attitude of either vessel changes the fact that the vessel originally overtaking is the give-way craft.

INTERNATIONAL RULE #14 - COMMENTS

When meeting head-on, bow to bow, come to the right to pass. If in doubt that a head-on collision situation exists, assume it does and act accordingly. Once again, keep your eye on Rule 2b.

RULE #15

Crossing Situation

When two power-driven vessels are crossing so as to involve risk of collision, the vessel which has the other on her own starboard side shall keep out of the way and shall, if the circumstances of the case admit, avoid crossing ahead of the other vessel.

RULE #16

Action By Give-Way Vessel

Every vessel which is directed to keep out of the way of another vessel shall, so far as possible, take early and substantial action to keep well clear.

RULE #17

Action By Stand-On Vessel

(a)(i) Where one of two vessels is to keep out of the way the other shall keep her course and speed.

(ii) The latter vessel may however take action to avoid collision by her maneuver alone, as soon as it becomes apparent to her that the vessel required to keep out of the way is not taking appropriate action in compliance with these Rules.

(b) When, from any cause, the vessel required to keep her course and speed finds herself so close that collision cannot be avoided by the action of the give-way vessel alone, she shall take such action as will best aid to avoid collision.

(c) A power-driven vessel which takes action in a crossing situation in accordance with sub-paragraph **(a)(ii)** of this Rule to avoid collision with another power-driven vessel shall, if the circumstances of the case admit, not alter course to port for a vessel on her own port side.

(d) This Rule does not relieve the give-way vessel of her obligation to keep out of the way.

INTERNATIONAL RULE #15 - COMMENTS

15) Very simple. The vessel off the starboard side of another craft is the stand-on craft. He has the right-of-way. Memory crutch. When you, or the other craft sees a green sidelight, that craft has the right-of-way.

Be sure and see the Inland Rule on this one. Quite a bit added and often found on Coast Guard license exams.

INTERNATIONAL RULE #16 - COMMENTS

Obvious. Do it soon, do it early, plan ahead and don't wait if you are the give-way craft.

INTERNATIONAL RULE #17 - COMMENTS

17a) If you have the right-of-way, if you are the stand-on craft, you are expected to maintain course and speed during the crossing situation. However, if it appears the other vessel is driven by an idiot unaware of the Rules, stay out of his way. Don't push your luck simply because you have the right-of-way.

17b) You must read between the maneuvers. Maybe a nearby sandspit, third vessel or a water-skiier is hampering the other vessel's maneuver to stay clear of you, the stand-on vessel. In such a case, it might take both of your actions to avoid a collision.

17c) Avoid turning left if the other craft is on your port side. This sounds simple, but it more critically defines a situation in a traffic or fairway problem.

17d) The give-way vessel, despite the stand-on vessel's maneuvers to avoid collision, is still the give-way vessel.

RULE #18

Responsibilities Between Vessels

Except where Rules 9, 10, and 13 otherwise require:
(a) A power-driven vessel underway shall keep out of the way of:
(i) a vessel not under command;
(ii) a vessel restricted in her ability to maneuver;
(iii) a vessel engaged in fishing;
(iv) a sailing vessel.

(b) A sailing vessel underway shall keep out of the way of:
(i) a vessel not under command;
(ii) a vessel restricted in her ability to maneuver;
(iii) a vessel engaged in fishing.

(c) A vessel engaged in fishing when underway shall, so far as possible, keep out of the way of:
(i) a vessel not under command;
(ii) a vessel restricted in her ability to maneuver.

(d)(i) Any vessel other than a vessel not under command or a vessel restricted in her ability to maneuver shall, if the circumstances of the case admit, avoid impeding the safe passage of a vessel constrained by her draft, exhibiting the signals in RULE 28.
(ii) A vessel constrained by her draft shall navigate with particular caution having full regard to her special condition.

(e) A seaplane on the water shall, in general, keep well clear of all vessels and avoid impeding their navigation. In circumstances, however, where risk of collision exists, she shall comply with the Rules of this Part.

INTERNATIONAL RULE #18 - COMMENTS

This is the famous (or infamous-depending on where you're sitting) pecking order. Who has the right-of-way over who? See page 102

License candidates should keep their minds on two significant differences between Inland and International in this context. Note that "trolling" is not considered fishing with the accompanying right-of-way of fishing vessels over sail and ordinary power boats. Secondly, Inland Rules do not recognize vessels "constrained by draft" i.e., deep draft vessels in narrow or shallow channels.

Other than the two exceptions cited above, International and Inland are the same in this Rule.

SECTION III-CONDUCT OF VESSELS IN RESTRICTED VISIBILITY

RULE #19

(a) This Rules applies to vessels not in sight of one another when navigating in or near an area of restricted visibility.

(b) Every vessel shall proceed at a safe speed adapted to the prevailing circumstances and conditions of restricted visibility. A power-driven vessel shall have her engines ready for immediate maneuver.

(c) Every vessel shall have due regard to the prevailing circumstances and conditions of restricted visibility when complying with **Section 1** of this part.

(d) A vessel which detects by radar the presence of another vessel shall determine if a close-quarters situation is developing and/or risk of collision exists. If so, she shall take avoiding action in ample time, provided that when such action consists of an alteration of course, so far as possible the following shall be avoided.

(i) an alteration of course to port for a vessel forward of the beam, other than for a vessel being overtaken;
(ii) an alteration of course towards a vessel abeam or abaft the beam.

(e) Except where it has been determined that a risk of collision does not exist, every vessel which hears apparently forward of her beam the fog signal of another vessel, or which cannot avoid a close-quarters situation with another vessel forward of her beam, shall reduce her speed to the minimum at which she can be kept on her course. She shall if necessary take all her way off and in any event navigate with extreme caution until danger of collision is over.

INTERNATIONAL RULE #19 - COMMENTS

19a) Restricted visibility! Not just fog. Bad storm, high seas, mist, falling snow, swarming locusts. And note the vessels are no longer in sight of one another which means Rules 11 through 18 **no longer apply.** Study the title to page 38. Some people never do get the implication here. Now we have **new** maneuvering rules...and whistle rules. Well, then if not new, certainly different.

19b) Safe speed-keep engines ready for some fast maneuvering. That doesn't necessarily mean come to a dead stop.

19c) The Rules in Section I still apply! Better study them again.

19d) Plan ahead with your radar-which if you carry and is operational, **must be in use in restricted visibility.** Plan ahead. If someone is ahead of you, don't turn left. If someone is abeam of aft of your beam, don't turn into them.

19e) Go slow. IF NECESSARY, take all way off and wait. Keep the fog signal going. Never use danger signal in restricted visibility.

Interesting. Here, for the first and only time, the term "fog signal" is used. Elsewhere it's called a "whistle signal." Would that make a good test question?

⚓

PART C-LIGHTS AND SHAPES

RULE #20

Application

(a) Rules in this Part shall be complied with in all weathers.

(b) The Rules concerning lights shall be complied with from sunset to sunrise, and during such times no other lights shall be exhibited, except such lights as cannot be mistaken for the lights specified in these Rules or do not impair their visibility or distinctive character, or interfere with the keeping of a proper look-out.

(c) The lights prescribed by these Rules shall, if carried, also be exhibited from sunrise to sunset in restricted visibility and may be exhibited in all other circumstances when it is deemed necessary.

(d) The Rules concerning shapes shall be complied with by day.

(e) The lights and shapes specified in these Rules shall comply with the provisions of Annex I to the Regulations.

INTERNATIONAL RULE #20 - COMMENTS

Almost all working vessels have special lights and dayshapes they display at appropriate times to indicate the nature of their marine work. The lights are 360 degree lights, thus they can be seen from any approach.

However, this rule is also concerned with the more simpler lights found on other commercial and pleasure craft such as the masthead lights, stern lights and side lights. These should be displayed whenever visibility becomes restricted in any way and from sunset to sunrise.

The special dayshapes are to be displayed during daylight. Far and away, most of the shapes are on working vessels, but not all. Sailboats with engines engaged beware.

If in doubt, turn on your running lights. See pages 90-99.

RULE #21

Definitions

(a) "Masthead light" means a white light placed over the fore and aft centerline of the vessel showing an unbroken light over an arc of the horizon of 225 degress and so fixed as to show the light from right ahead to 22.5 degrees abaft the beam on either side of the vessel.

(b) "Sidelights" means a green light on the starboard side and a red light on the port side each showing an unbroken light over an arc of the horizon of 112.5 degrees and so fixed as to show the light from right ahead to 22.5 degrees abaft the beam on its respective side. In a vessel of less than 20 meters in length the sidelights may be combined in one lantern carried on the fore and aft centerline of the vessel.

(c) "Sternlight" means a white light placed as nearly as practicable at the stern showing an unbroken light over an arc of the horizon of 135 degrees and so fixed as to show the light 67.5 degrees from right aft on each side of the vessel.

(d) "Towing light" means a yellow light having the same characteristics as the "sternlight" defined in **paragraph (c)** of this Rule.

(e) "All-round light" means a light showing an unbroken light over an arc of the horizon of 360 degrees.

(f) "Flashing light" means a light flashing at regular intervals at a frequency of 120 flashes or more per minute.

INTERNATIONAL RULE #21 - COMMENTS

A brief summary of on-board lights and their respective arcs follows.

1) Masthead lights shine 225 degrees. That is, 112.5 degrees on each side. See pages 100-101.

2) Sidelights are red on the port side and green on the starboard side. Each sidelight shines from dead ahead to 22.5 degrees abaft each beam. Another way of putting it is that each sidelight shines from dead ahead for an arc of 112.5 degrees on each side of the vessel. **NOTE** - Sidelights have a **combined** arc of 225 degrees which is the same as a masthead light. In short, if you can see the masthead light, you can see at least one of the sidelights.

3) All sternlights shine 135 degrees aft. That is, 67.5 dgrees on each side. Since a full circle has 360 degrees this means you can see the sternlight, but when you do you won't see either sidelight or the masthead light. The opposite is also true. 135 + 225 = 360.

4) A towing light is yellow. When used, it's always on the stern and always the same arc as the traditional sternlight; 135 degrees. On International waters this means the vessel with this light (among others) is towing astern, alongside or pushing ahead. The towing light displayed on Inland waters differs. Be sure and read Comments under Inland Rule 21 so you have it straight. Guaranteed to be on your Rules of The Road module in one form or another.

5) The so-called "all-round light" is simply a 360 degree light. Not necessarily always white. See Rule 23 for some applications.

6) This bit about a "flashing light" can be confusing because in Inland waters they have all of the above plus a "special flashing light" they use on barges when the barge is being pushed ahead of the tow. Anyway, get the timing down.

RULE #22

Visibility of Lights

The lights prescribed in these Rules shall have an intensity as specified in Section 8 of Annex I to these Regulations so as to be visible at the following minimum ranges:

(a) In vessels of 50 meters or more in length:
- -a masthead light, 6 miles;
- -a sidelight, 3 miles;
- -a sternlight, 3 miles;
- -a towing light, 3 miles;
- -a white, red, green or yellow all-round light, 3 miles.

(b) In vessels of 12 meters or more in length but less than 50 meters in length:
- -a masthead light, 5 miles; except that where the length of the vessel is less than 20 meters, 3 miles;
- -a sidelight, 2 miles;
- -a sternlight, 2 miles;
- -a towing light, 2 miles;
- -a white, red, green or yellow all-round light, 2 miles.

(c) In vessels of less than 12 meters in length:
- -a masthead light, 2 miles;
- -a sidelight, 1 mile;
- -a sternlight, 2 miles;
- -a towing light, 2 miles;
- -a white, red, green or yellow all-round light, 2 miles.

(d) In inconspicuous, partly submerged vessels or objects being towed:
- -a white all-round light, 3 miles.

INTERNATIONAL RULE #22 - COMMENTS

For a pictorial representation of the entire subject, see pages 100-101.

For serious mariners preparing to renew, upgrade or sit for original licenses consider our flashcards. They include not simply the lights and dayshapes, but maneuvering sound signals, signals in restricted visibility and study cards for the arcs and visibility of lights.

An order form is in the back of this volume.

RULE #23

Power-Driven Vessels Underway

(a) A power-driven vessel underway shall exhibit:

(i) a masthead light forward;

(ii) a second masthead light abaft of and higher than the forward one; except that a vessel of less than 50 meters in length shall not be obliged to exhibit such a light may do so;

(iii) sidelights;

(iv) a sternlight.

(b) An air-cushion vessel when operating in the non-displacement mode shall, in addition to the lights prescribed in **paragraph (a)** of this Rule, exhibit an all-round flashing yellow light.

(c)(i) A power-driven vessel of less than 12 meters in length may, in lieu of the lights prescribed in **paragraph (a)** of this Rule, exhibit an all-round white light and sidelights.

(ii) a power-driven vessel of less than 7 meters in length whose maximum speed does not exceed 7 knots may, in lieu of the lights prescribed in **paragraph (a)** of this Rule, exhibit an all-round white light, and shall if practicable, also exhibit sidelights;

(iii) the masthead light or all-round white light on a power-driven vessel of less than 12 meters in length may be displaced from the fore and aft centerline of the vessel if centerline fitting is not practicable, provided that the sidelights are combined in one lantern which shall be carried on the fore and aft centerline of the vessel or located as nearly as practicable in the same fore and aft line as the masthead light or the all-round white light.

INTERNATIONAL RULE #23 - COMMENTS

Now that we know the arcs of the four types of lights, - masthead, sidelights, sternlights and towing lights- we need to know where they go on the various vessels. This is indicated on Comments in the Inland and International Rule 22 and pages 100-101, but some variations are worth mentioning.

23a) Basically, vessels less than 50 meters in length need only show one masthead light forward. Fifty meters or greater **must have** an additional masthead light aft and the after one must be higher than the forward light.

23b) Air-cushion vessels need to add a flashing yellow light.

23c) Power vessels less than 12 meters in length can use an all-round white light instead of a masthead light, but still need to show sidelights, (see pages 90-91). The all-round white light can be off-center but it and the sidelights should be on the same fore and aft line. It's all a matter of convenience.

If less than 7 meters and making less than 7 knots the power vessel still needs the all round white light, but can get away without sidelights if not "practicable." Also found on pages 90-91.

RULE #24

Towing and Pushing

(a) A power-driven vessel when towing shall exhibit:
(i) instead of the light prescribed in **Rule 23(a)(i)** or **(a)(ii)**, two masthead lights in a vertical line. When the length of the tow, measuring from the stern of the towing vessel to the after end of the tow exceeds 200 meters, three such lights in a vertical line;
(ii) sidelights;
(iii) a sternlight;
(iv) a towing light in a vertical line above the sternlight;
(v) when the length of the tow exceeds 200 meters, a diamond shape where it can best be seen.

(b) When a pushing vessel and a vessel being pushed ahead are rigidly connected in a composite unit they shall be regarded as a power-driven vessel and exhibit the lights prescribed in **Rule 23.**

(c) A power-driven vessel when pushing ahead or towing alongside, except in the case of a composite unit, shall exhibit:
(i) instead of the light prescribed in **Rule 23(a)(i)** or **(a)(ii)**, two masthead lights in a vertical line;
(ii) sidelights;
(iii) a sternlight.

(d) A power-driven vessel to which **paragraph (a)** or **(c)** of this Rule apply shall also comply with Rule **23(a)(ii)**.

(e) A vessel or object being towed, other than those mentioned in **paragraph (g)** of this Rule, shall exhibit:
(i) sidelights;
(ii) a sternlight;
(iii) when the length of the tow exceeds 200 meters, a diamond shape where it can best be seen.

(Cont'd)

INTERNATIONAL RULE #24 - COMMENTS

24a-f) A summary of International towing is depicted on pages 92-93. **TUGS** come in two categories: Short (less than 50 meters in length) and Long (50 meters or greater.) **TOWS** come in two categories: Short-less than 200 meters astern and Long-200 meters or greater astern. In International waters tugs use the same lights whether towing behind, alongside or pushing ahead. When you have this straight, go study the Inland version. Quite a difference. See also pages 98-99.

(Cont'd)

RULE #24 (Cont'd)

(f) Provided that any number of vessels being towed alongside or pushed in a group shall be lighted as one vessel,

(i) a vessel being pushed ahead, not being part of a composite unit, shall exhibit at the forward end, sidelights;

(ii) a vessel being towed alongside shall exhibit a sternlight and at the forward end, sidelights.

(g) An inconspicuous, partly submerged vessel or object, or combination of such vessels or objects being towed, shall exhibit:

(i) if it is less than 25 meters in breadth, one all-round white light at or near the forward end and one at or near the after end except that dracones need not exhibit a light at or near the forward end;

(ii) if it is 25 meters or more in breadth, two additional all-round white lights at or near the extremities of its' breadth;

(iii) if it exceeds 100 meters in length, additional all-round white lights between the lights prescribed in **subparagraphs (i)** and **(ii)** so that the distance between the lights shall not exceed 100 meters;

(iv) A diamond shape at or near the aftermost extremity of the last vessel or object being towed; and if the length of the tow exceeds 200 meters an additional diamond shape where it can best be seen and located as far forward as is practicable.

(Cont'd)

INTERNATIONAL RULE #24 - COMMENTS

24g) A submerged, or partially submerged object in tow requires lights. A dracone does not. A dracone is a plastic-like or rubber bladder, presumably loaded with some chemical, oil or other petroleum. For lights on barges see pages 98-99. Then recall how barges are lighted with sidelights and sternlights when towed or pushed in groups.

24h) If it can't be lighted, shine a light on it when other craft approach.

(Cont'd)

RULE #24 (Cont'd)

(h) Where from any sufficient cause it is impracticable for a vessel or object being towed to exhibit the lights or shapes prescribed in **paragraph (e)** or **(g)** of this Rule, all possible measures shall be taken to light the vessel or object towed or at least to indicate the presence of such vessel or object.

(i) Where from any sufficient cause it is impracticable for a vessel not normally engaged in towing operations to display the lights prescribed in paragraph (a) or (c) of this Rule, such vessels shall not be required to exhibit those lights when engaged in towing another vessel in distress or otherwise in need of assistance. All possible measures shall be taken to indicate the nature of the relationship between the towing vessel and the vessel being towed as authorized by **Rule 36**, in particular by illuminating the towline.

INTERNATIONAL RULE #24 - COMMENTS

24i) An amateur towing in a disabled craft need not light up like a commercial tug. But, be able to indicate the tow to others on the approach.

Incidentally, lights and dayshapes like the big guys wear, the commercial vessels hard at their respective tasks, like underwater work, buoy tending and landing aircraft, are not worn by small non-commercial vessels. There is the one exception.

Even non-commercial diveboats should show the rigidly constructed alfa flag by day when divers are down or the three vertically arranged lights indicating restricted in ability to maneuver, i.e. red-over-white-over-red when on night dives. See pages 96-97.

▶⚓◀

RULE #25

Sailing Vessels Underway and Vessels Under Oars

(a) A sailing vessel underway shall exhibit:
(i) sidelights;
(ii) a sternlight.

(b) In a sailing vessel of less than 20 meters in length the lights prescribed in paragraph (a) of this Rule may be combined in one lantern carried at or near the top of the mast where it can best be seen.

(c) A sailing vessel underway may, in addition to the lights prescribed in paragraph (a) of this Rule, exhibit at or near the top of the mast, where they can best be seen, two all-round lights in a vertical line, the upper being red and the lower green, but these lights shall not be exhibited in conjunction with the combined lantern permitted by paragraph (b) of this Rule.

(d) A sailing vessel of less than 7 meters in length shall, if practicable, exhibit the lights prescribed in paragraph (a) or (b) of this Rule, but if she does not, she shall have ready at hand an electric torch or lighted lantern showing a white light which shall be exhibited in sufficient time to prevent collision.

(ii) A vessel under oars may exhibit the lights prescribed in this Rule for sailing vessels, but if she does not, she shall have ready at hand an electric torch or lighted lantern showing a white light which shall be exhibited in sufficient time to prevent collision.

(e) A vessel proceeding under sail when also being propelled by machinery shall exhibit forward where it can best be seen a conical shape, apex downwards. ▼

INTERNATIONAL RULE #25 - COMMENTS

25a-c) Sailboats always need at least a sternlight and sidelights. If the sailboat is less than 20 meters in length a combination sternlight and sidelights can be carried atop the mast. If this option is taken, another option must be surrendered-that of displaying a red over a green 360 degree light high on the mast.

25d) Sailboats less than 7 meters in length can get away without showing stern and sidelights, but must have a flashlight handy to ward off on-coming craft. The same lights are required for a rowboat, including the option of the flashlight. For this and above-see pages 90-91.

RULE #26

Fishing Vessels

(a) A vessel engaged in fishing, whether underway or at anchor, shall exhibit only the lights and shapes prescribed in this Rule.

(b) A vessel when engaged in trawling, by which is meant the dragging through the water of a dredge net or other apparatus used as a fishing appliance, shall exhibit:
(i) two all-round lights in a vertical line, the upper being green and the lower white, or a shape consisting of two cones with their apexes together in a vertical line one above the other; a vessel less than 20 meters in length may instead of this shape exhibit a basket;
(ii) a masthead light abaft of and higher than the all-round green light; a vessel of less than 50 meters in length shall not be obliged to exhibit such a light but may do so;
(iii) when making way through the water, in addition to the lights prescribed in this paragraph, sidelights and a sternlight.

(c) A vessel engaged in fishing, other than trawling, shall exhibit:
(i) two all-round lights in a vertical line, the upper being red and the lower white, or a shape consisting of two cones with apexes together in a vertical line one above the other; a vessel of less than 20 meters in length may instead of this shape exhibit a basket;
(ii) when there is outlying gear extending more than 150 meters horizontally from the vessel, an all-round white light or a cone apex upwards in the direction of the gear;
(iii) when making way through the water, in addition to the lights prescribed in this paragraph, sidelights and a sternlight.

(d) A vessel engaged in fishing in close proximity to other vessels engaged in fishing may exhibit the additional signals described in Annex II to these Regulations.

(e) A vessel when not engaged in fishing shall not exhibit the lights or shapes prescribed in this Rule, but only those prescribed for a vessel of her length.

INTERNATIONAL RULE #26 - COMMENTS

Careful here. CG test modules have some tricky ones on fishing vessels built around the following facts: See pages 96-97

26a-b) Recalling that all special lights show 360 degrees, the trawler shows green over white on the mast. Also, **when making way,** sidelights and a sternlight. Masthead lights apply. One forward for less than 50 meters (as usual) and one aft if 50 meters or greater in length. Big point: Sidelights and sternlights are used only when underway. Since the fishing vessel shows only those lights prescribed here-this means they show no anchor light when fishing at anchor.

26c) Fishing vessel with lines or nets shows red over white at the mast. The dayshape for fishing and trawling is the double cone, point to point. If less than 20 meters **can** use a basket. And again, when underway, turn on the side and sternlights. Remember, the fishing vessel can be fishing when underway with no way on, when underway with way on and when at anchor.

26d) Special lights when fishing close-in and/or in a team. These are detailed in Annex II, but basically: Purseiners show two yellow lights, vertically arranged and flashing alternately every second. Trawlers can use a searchlight to point out the other ship with which they are fishing. Trawlers also have special vertically arranged lights to indicate the action they are currently taking with their nets. White over white=shooting the nets; white over red=hauling the nets; and red over red means they are hung up on an obstruction, presumably a rock or the like and are having trouble pulling their nets.

Two terms important here: Demersal fishing is a fancy word meaning the nets sink to the bottom as with the more traditional trawler. Pelagic means the nets being hauled from the craft and are afloat, i.e., not bottom fishing.

RULE 27

Vessels Not Under Command or Restricted In Their Ability to Maneuver

(a) A vessel not under command shall exhibit:

(i) two all-round red lights in a vertical line where they can best be seen;

(ii) two balls or similar shapes in a vertical line where they can best be seen;

(iii) when making way through the water, in addition to the lights prescribed in this paragraph, sidelights and a sternlight.

(b) A vessel restricted in her ability to maneuver, except a vessel engaged in mineclearance operations, shall exhibit:

(i) three all-round lights in a vertical line where they can best be seen. The highest and lowest of these lights shall be red and the middle light shall be white;

(ii) three shapes in a vertical line where they can best be seen. The highest and lowest of these shapes shall be balls and the middle one a diamond.

(iii) when making way through the water, a masthead light or lights, sidelights and a sternlight, in addition to the lights prescribed in subparagraph **(i)**;

(iv) when at anchor, in addition to the lights or shapes prescribed in **subparagraphs (i)** and **(ii)**, the light, lights or shape prescribed in **Rule 30.**

(c) A power-driven vessel engaged in a towing operation such as severely restricts the towing vessel and her tow in their ability to deviate from their course shall, in addition to the lights or shapes prescribed in **Rule 24(a)**, exhibit the lights or shapes prescribed in **subparagraphs (b)(i)** and **(ii)** of this Rule.

(Cont'd)

INTERNATIONAL RULE #27 - COMMENTS

This Rule covers two separate types of "working" craft, both of which are listed in the Pecking Order found in Rule and Comments-Rule 18. See also page 102.

Not under command means being adrift. She may have power, but maybe she can't steer or maneuver effectively. Top priority on the pecking order. Night will find her showing two red lights, vertically arranged. Like all special lights they are 360 degrees. Dayshape is two black balls. Pages 96-97.

Aground is also not under command. Now, to the red over red lights is added an anchor light, or two anchor lights if 50 meters or greater in length. The dayshape changes to three black balls. Often on exams. And don't let the dayshapes throw you. They are simply cut from metal sheets and displayed aloft.

Number two on the pecking order is "Restricted In Ability to Maneuver," but includes almost everyone working when maneuvering is difficult. Again, see the summary art work on Rule 18 Comments. The signal at night is red-over-white-over red. The dayshape is ball-diamond-ball. With the exception of the alfa flag and the fishing basket, all dayshapes are black. Pages 94-95.

The minesweeper shows three green lights: One from the top of the mast and one each on each end of the top-most yard. Daylight finds the green lights replaced by black balls, same locations. Pages 94-95.

(Cont'd)

RULE 27 (Con't)

(d) A vessel engaged in dredging or underwater operations when restricted in her ability to maneuver, shall exhibit the lights and shapes prescribed in **subparagraphs (b)(i), (ii)** and **(iii)** of the Rule and shall in addition, when an obstruction exists, exhibit:

(i) two all-round red lights or two balls in a vertical line to indicate the side on which the obstruction exists;

(ii) two all-round green lights or two diamonds in a vertical line to indicate the side on which another vessel may pass;

(iii) when at anchor, the lights or shapes prescribed in this paragraph instead of the lights or shape prescribed in **Rule 30**, for anchored vessels.

(e) Whenever the size of a vessel engaged in diving operations makes it impracticable to exhibit all lights and shapes prescribed in paragraph **(d)** of this Rule, the following shall be exhibited:

(i) three all-round lights in a vertical line where they can best be seen. The highest and lowest of these lights shall be red and the middle light shall be white;

(ii) a rigid replica of the International Code flag "A" not less than 1 meter in height. Measures shall be taken to ensure its' all-round visibility.

(f) A vessel engaged in mineclearance operations shall in addition to the lights prescribed for a power-driven vessel in **Rule 23** or to the lights or shape prescribed for a vessel at anchore in **Rule 30** as appropriate, exhibit three all-round green lights or three balls. One of these lights or shapes shall be exhibited near the foremast head and one at each end of the fore yard. These lights or shapes indicate that it is dangerous for another vessel to approach within 1000 meters or the mineclearance vessel.

(Cont'd)

(Cont'd)

For tug lights and definitions, see Rule 24 and pp. 92-93 and 98-99 noting very carefully the difference in lights between Inland and International tugs pushing and towing alongside.

Vessels engaged in underwater work show two black balls (dayshapes) or two red lights (night) over the working obstructed side. The passing side shows two black diamonds or two green lights-all of which are vertically arranged. Recall all of these "restricted in ability to maneuver" vessels **also show** red-over-white-over-red vertically arranged lights or the black ball-diamond-ball dayshape. Pages 94-95

Vessels less than 12 meters-except dive boats, need not carry these signals. The dayshape for the dive flag is the International Code flag "A", or alfa. Pages 96-97.

RULE #27 (Cont'd)

(g) Vessels of less than 12 meters in length, except those engaged in diving operations, shall not be required to exhibit the lights and shapes prescribed in this Rule.

(h) The signals prescribed in this Rule are not signals of vessels in distress and requiring assistance. Such signals are contained in **Annex IV** to these Regulations.

RULE #28

Vessels Constrained By Their Draft

A vessel constrained by her draft may, in addition to the lights prescribed for power-driven vessels in **Rule 23,** exhibit where they can best be seen three all-round red lights in a vertical line, or a cylinder.

RULE #29

Pilot Vessels

29(a) A vessel engaged on pilotage duty shall exhibit:

(i) at or near the masthead, two all-round lights in a vertical line, the upper being white and the lower red;

(ii) when underway, in addition, sidelights and a sternlight;

(iii) when at anchor, in addition to the lights prescribed in **subparagraph (i)**, the light, lights or shape prescribed in **Rule 30** for vessels at anchor.

(b) A pilot vessel when not engaged on pilotage duty shall exhibit the lights or shapes prescribed for a similar vessel of her length.

INTERNATIONAL RULE #28 - COMMENTS

Vessels constrained by their draft, meaning they are operating in a shallow and/or narrow channel and hence are severely restricted in maneuverability have special lights in International waters. Three red lights, 360 degrees and vertically arranged. The dayshape is a black cylinder. There is no such signal on inland waters. See pages 96-97 & 102.

INLAND RULE #29 - COMMENTS

The night signal for a pilot vessel is white over red. Opposite that of fishing. "White over red, pilot ahead," is an old memory crutch. There is no dayshape. At anchor, she must use anchor lights. When not on duty, she may not display these identification lights. See pages 98-99.

RULE #30

Anchored Vessels and Vessels Aground

(a) A vessel at anchor shall exhibit where it can best be seen:
(i) in the fore part, an all-round white light or one ball;
(ii) at or near the stern and at a lower level than the light prescribed in **subparagraph (i)**, an all-round white light.

(b) A vessel of less than 50 meters in length may exhibit an all-round white light where it can best be seen instead of the lights prescribed in **paragraph (a)** of this Rule.

(c) A vessel at anchor may, and a vessel of 100 meters and more in length shall, also use the available working or equivalent lights to illuminate her decks.

(d) A vessel aground shall exhibit the lights prescribed in **paragraph (a)** or **(b)** of this Rule and in addition, where they can best be seen:
(i) two all-round red lights in a vertical line;
(ii) three balls in a vertical line.

(e) A vessel of less than 7 meters in length, when at anchor, not in or near a narrow channel, fairway or anchorage, or where other vessels normally navigate, shall not be required to exhibit the lights or shape prescribed in **paragraphs (a)** and **(b)** of this Rule.

(f) A vessel of less than 12 meters in length, when aground, shall not be required to exhibit the lights or shapes prescribed in **subparagraphs (d)(i)** and **(ii)** of this Rule.

RULE #31

Seaplanes

Where it is impracticable for a seaplane to exhibit lights and shapes of the characteristics or in the positions prescribed in the Rules of this Part she shall exhibit lights and shapes as closely similar in characteristics and position as is possible.

INTERNATIONAL RULE #30 - COMMENTS

Basically, anchored vessels fall into three memory categories. (1) If at anchor a black ball forward for a dayshape, (2) or at night, one white light forward if less than 50 meters in length. (3) If 50 meters of more in length, two white lights at night, the after one lower than the forward one. This vertical positioning fore and aft is opposite that of masthead lights whereby the lower light is forward, the after one higher when underway. Pages 94-95.

Vessels 100 meters or greater in length should illuminate their decks in addition to the above signals.

Recall that a vessel aground shows the red-over-red of a vessel not under command **as well as** the dayshape of three black balls instead of the single anchor ball. Also, when aground she shows the anchor lights indicated above.

Vessels less than 12 meters in length, when **aground**, need not show these signals above. Even vessels less than 7 meters in length, when **anchored** in out-of-the-way inlets, coves where traffic is normally almost non-existant, need not show the anchor signals above.

Be sure to see the slight Inland difference.

INTERNATIONAL RULE #31 - COMMENTS

Simple and obvious. No comments needed.

PART D - SOUND AND LIGHT SIGNALS

RULE #32

Definitions

(a) The word "whistle" means any sound signalling appliance capable of producing the prescribed blasts and which complies with the specifications in **Annex III** to these Regulations.

(b) The term "short blast" means a blast of about one seconds' duration.

(c) The term "prolonged blast" means a blast of from four to six seconds' duration.

RULE #33

Equipment for Sound Signals

(a) A vessel of 12 meters or more in length shall be provided with a whistle and a bell and a vessel of 100 meters or more in length shall, in addition, be provided with a gong, the tone and sound of which cannot be confused with that of the bell. The whistle, bell and gong shall comply with the specifications in **Annex III** to these Regulations. The bell or gong or both may be replaced by other equipment having the same respective sound characteristics, provided that manual sounding of the prescribed signals shall always be possible.

(b) A vessel of less than 12 meters in length shall not be obliged to carry the sound signalling appliances prescribed in **paragraph (a)** of this Rule but if she does not, she shall be provided with some other means of making an efficient sound signal.

INTERNATIONAL RULE #32 - COMMENTS

Another obvious one. Remember the whistle blast durations.

INTERNATIONAL RULE #33 - COMMENTS

Everyone has to be able to make a sound signal to attract attention in restricted visibility and when maneuvering.

Vessels less than 12 meters can use any "sound producing mechanism" that works and gets the job done by attracting attention. Some use freon horns (but not for much longer), police whistles and loud rattling instruments. In some harbors and yacht clubs there is competition to see who can come up with the most ingenious...or ridiculous. Depends on whether you live in Massachusetts or California

Vessels 12 meters or more in length must have on board at all times a bell and a whistle. Vessels 100 meters or more in length must also carry a gong. The gong is for anchoring or going aground in a fog. Good for laughs in Rule 35.

RULE #34

Maneuvering and Warning Signals

(a) When vessels are in sight of one another, a power-driven vessel underway, when maneuvering as authorized or required by these Rules, shall indicate that maneuver by the following signals on her whistle:

one short blast to mean "I am altering my course to starboard";

two short blasts to mean "I am altering my course to port";

three short blasts to mean "I am operating astern propulsion".

(b) Any vessel may supplement the whistle signals prescribed in **paragraph (a)** of this Rule by light signals, repeated as appropriate, whilst the maneuver is being carried out:

(i) these light signals shall have the following significance:

one flash to mean "I am altering my course to starboard";

two flashes to mean "I am altering my course to port";

three flashes to mean "I am operating astern propulsion";

(ii) the duration of each flash shall be about one second, the interval between flashes shall be about one second, and the interval between successive signals shall be not less than ten seconds;

(iii) the light used for this signal shall, if fitted, be an all-round white light, visible at a minimum range of 5 miles, and shall comply with the provisions of **Annex I** to these Regulations.

(Cont'd)

INTERNATIONAL RULE #34 - COMMENTS

These signals are given in International waters when vessels are within sight of each other. In Inland waters the signals are given when vessels are within sight of each other **and when within a half-mile** of each other.

Herein lies one critical difference between International and Inland Rules. Note the whistle signals in the International context mean that when the signal is sounded **by** the **give-way** power-driven vessels the maneuver is already in progress. The maneuver **IS BEING CARRIED OUT.** Furthermore, no return signal from the **stand-on** craft is necessary. Another way of putting it is: if the vessel on International waters need not change course, no one or two blast signal is necessary.

This is not the case Inland. The whistle signals Inland mean you **intend** to execute a given maneuver. The stand-on vessel, upon hearing **either one or two blasts** from the give-way craft then **returns** the signal. **Then and only then, is the maneuver carried out.** See page 89.

Again-in both Inland and International, the maneuvering signals are first sounded by the give-way craft.

An exception to this is in Inland waters when the down-bound vessel **with a following current** has the right of way, is expected to sound the signals and choose the manner of crossing, overtaking, etc.

(Cont'd)

RULE #34 (Cont'd)

(c) When in sight of one another in a narrow channel or fairway:

(i) a vessel intending to overtake another shall in compliance with **Rule 9(e)(i)** indicate her intention by the following signals on her whistle:

-two prolonged blasts followed by one short blast to mean "I intend to overtake you on your starboard side";

-two prolonged blasts followed by two short blasts to mean "I intend to overtake you on your port side".

(ii) the vessel about to be overtaken when acting in accordance with **Rule 9 (e)(i)** shall indicate her agreement by the following signal on her whistle:

-one prolonged, one short, one prolonged and one short blast, in that order.

(d) When vessels in sight of one another are approaching each other and from any cause either vessel fails to understand the intentions or actions of the other, or is in doubt whether sufficient action is being taken by the other to avoid collision, the vessel in doubt shall immediately indicate such doubt by giving at least five short and rapid blasts on the whistle. Such signal may be supplemented by a light signal of at least five short and rapid flashes.

(e) A vessel nearing a bend or an area of a channel or fairway where other vessels may be obscured by an intervening obstruction shall sound one prolonged blast. Such signal shall be answered with a prolonged blast by any approaching vessel that may be within hearing around the bend or behind the intervening obstruction.

(f) If whistles are fitted on a vessel at a distance apart of more than 100 meters, one whistle only shall be used for giving maneuvering and warning signals.

(Cont'd)

INTERNATIONAL RULE #34 - COMMENTS

NOTE: There is a signal for overtaking in a narrow channel in International waters not found in Inland waters. Also, on Inland waters, a vessel getting underway from a dock, pier or other mooring must sound one prolonged blast. Not cited in International Rules.

The one prolonged blast is also sounded both Inland and International when vessels are approaching channel bends or intervening obstructions. This signal is returned by anyone on the opposite approach. A CG test once observed that getting away from a dock, pier, wharf, etc., in International waters can be construed as being among "intervening obstructions" hence the prolonged blast is also needed for that reason in International waters!

Any maneuver, Inland or International, can be aborted by **any** vessel by sounding five or more short blasts on the whistle. The danger signal. The doubt signal.

These sound signals may be **supplemented** by light signals. But notice, the light used International is an all-round white light, but Inland is an all-round **yellow or white** light. An entire Rules of The Road quiz can be generated from the information relating to Rule 34.

On Inland waters the radiotelephone can be substituted for maneuvering signals. Not on International waters. Remember - All of the signals in Rule 34 pertain to **power-driven** vessels...not sailboats. See page 89 for a summary.

RULE #35

Sound Signals in Restricted Visibility

In or near an area of restricted visibility, whether by day or night, the signals prescribed in this Rule shall be used as follows:

(a) A power-driven vessel making way through the water shall sound at intervals of not more than 2 minutes one prolonged blast.

(b) A power-driven vessel underway but stopped and making no way through the water shall sound at intervals of not more than 2 minutes two prolonged blasts in succession with an interval of about 2 seconds between them.

(c) A vessel not under command, a vessel restricted in her ability to maneuver, a vessel constrained by her draft, a sailing vessel, a vessel engaged in fishing and a vessel engaged in towing or pushing another vessel shall, instead of the signals prescribed in **paragraphs (a)** or **(b)** of this Rule, sound at intervals of not more than 2 minutes three blasts in succession, namely one prolonged followed by two short blasts.

(d) A vessel engaged in fishing, when at anchor, and a vessel restricted in her ability to maneuver when carrying out her work at anchor, shall instead of the signals prescribed in **paragraph (g)** of this Rule sound the signal prescribed in **paragraph (c)** of this Rule.

(e) A vessel towed or if more than one vessel is towed the last vessel of the tow, if manned, shall at intervals of not more than 2 minutes sound four blasts in succession, namely one prolonged followed by three short blasts. When practicable, this signal shall be made immediately after the signal made by the towing vessel.

(Cont'd)

INTERNATIONAL RULE #35 - COMMENTS

A point often forgotten is that when moving into the realm of "restricted visibility" and especially dealing with sound signals, one must read again the titles to Section II commencing with Rule 11 and Part D commencing with Rule 32. The emphasis is that some signals are valid when vessels are within sight of each other, some in any condition visibility and now these-sound signals in restricted visibility.

The point is this: The usual maneuvering signals are not sounded in restricted visibility. The danger (doubt) signal is not sounded in restricted visibility. Instead, a new set of signals and maneuvering conduct is available. The signals indicated here were taken from: *The Coast Guard License-From Six Pac to Master 100 Tons* and represent a summary of the sounds to be given in restricted visibility. See also page 103.

If you would be interested in our Coast Guard license book please see the order form on the last page of this volume.

RULE #35 (Cont'd)

(f) When a pushing vessel and a vessel being pushed ahead are rigidly connected in a composite unit they shall be regarded as a power-driven vessel and shall give the signals prescribed in **paragraphs (a)** or **(b)** of this Rule.

(g) A vessel at anchor shall at intervals of not more than 1 minute ring the bell rapidly for about 5 seconds. In a vessel of 100 meters or more in length the bell shall be sounded in the forepart of the vessel and immediately after the ringing of the bell the gong shall be sounded rapidly for about 5 seconds in the after part of the vessel. A vessel at anchor may in addition sound three blasts in succession, namely one short, one prolonged and one short blast, to give warning of her position and of the possibility of collision to an approaching vessel.

(h) A vessel aground shall give the bell signal and if required the gong signal prescribed in **paragraph (g)** of this Rule and shall, in addition, give three separate and distinct strokes on the bell immediately before and after the rapid ringing of the bell. A vessel aground may in addition sound an appropriate whistle signal.

(i) A vessel of less than 12 meters in length shall not be obliged to give the above-mentioned signals but, if she does not, shall make some other efficient sound signal at intervals of not more than 2 minutes.

(j) A pilot vessel engaged on pilotage duty may in addition to the signals prescribed in **paragraphs (a)**, **(b)** or **(g)** of this Rule sound an identity signal consisting of four short blasts.

INTERNATIONAL RULE #35 - COMMENTS

For a condensed version of signals sounded in restricted visibility see page 103.

RULE #36

Signals to Attract Attention

If necessary to attract the attention of another vessel, any vessel may make light or sound signals that cannot be mistaken for any signal authorized elsewhere in these Rules, or may direct the beam of her searchlight in the direction of the danger, in such a way as not to embarrass any vessel. Any light to attract the attention of another vessel shall be such that it cannot be mistaken for any aid to navigation. For the purpose of this Rule the use of high intensity intermittent or revolving lights, such as strobe lights, shall be avoided.

RULE #37

Distress Signals

When a vessel is in distress and requires assistance she shall use or exhibit the signals described in Annex IV to these Regulations.

INTERNATIONAL RULE #36 - COMMENTS

Need to attract attention? Okay, just stay away from strobe lights and try not to shine your light into the pilot house of adjacent ships at night. This makes it tough on night vision. That's what "embarrass" means.

INTERNATIONAL RULE #37 - COMMENTS

The distress signals are indicated on page 104.

PART E - EXEMPTIONS

RULE #38

Exemptions

Any vessel (or class of vessels) provided that she complies with the requirements of the International Regulations for Preventing Collisions at Sea, 1960, the keel of which is laid or which is at a corresponding stage of construction before the entry into force of these Regulations may be exempted from compliance therewith as follows:

(a) The installation of lights with ranges prescribed in **Rule 22**, until four years after the date of entry into force of these Regulations.

(b) The installation of lights with color specifications as prescribed in **Section 7 of Annex I** to these Regulations, until four years after the date of entry into force of these Regulations.

(c) The repositioning of lights as a result of conversion from Imperial to metric units and rounding off measurement figures, permanent exemption.

(d)(i) The repositioning of masthead lights on vessels of less than 150 meters in length, resulting from the prescriptions of **Section 3(a) of Annex I** to these Regulations, permanent exemption.

(ii) The repositioning of masthead lights on vessels of 150 meters or more in length, resulting from the prescriptions of **Section 3(a) of Annex I** to these Regulations, until 9 years after the date of entry into force of these Regulations.

(e) The repositioning of masthead lights resulting from the prescriptions of **Section 2(b) of Annex I** to these Regulations, until 9 years after the date of entry into force of these Regulations.

(Cont'd)

INTERNATIONAL RULE #38 - COMMENTS

The exemptions detailed here speak for themselves, but boat owners in doubt are advised to contact the Coast Guard direct for a clearer picture. Always remember; don't buy advice from the Coast Guard, or for that matter from any other bureaucratic organization, over the phone. Get it in writing.

RULE #38 (Cont'd)

(f) The repositioning of sidelights resulting from the prescriptions of **Sections 2(g) and 3(b) of Annex I** to these Regulations, until 9 years after the date of entry into force of these Regulations.

(g) The requirements for sound signal appliances prescribed in **Annex III** to these Regulations, until 9 years after the date of entry into force of these Regulations.

(h) The repositioning of all-round lights resulting from the prescription of **Section 9(b) of Annex I** to these Regulations, permanent exemption.

INTERNATIONAL

HEAD ON

One Short Blast - I **AM** altering my course to starboard to pass port side to.

Two Short Blasts - I **AM** altering my course to port.

Three Short Blasts - I **AM** operating in astern propulsion.

CROSSING

One Short Blast - Initiated by the give-way craft indicating she **IS** altering course to starboard to pass astern of the on-coming craft, or is slowing to allow other vessel to maintain course & speed **which is the duty of the stand-on craft.**

OVERTAKING

One Short Blast - Altering course to starboard to overtake vessel ahead. If "danger" signal is sounded, abort maneuver and try again later.

Two Short Blasts - Same as above but vessel overtaking is coming left to pass.

OVERTAKING IN A NARROW CHANNEL

Two Prolonged - One Short. Given by the overtaking vessel in a narrow channel when the overtaking craft wishes to pass the vessel ahead by coming **right** and passing to the other vessel's starboard side.

Two Prolonged - Two Short. Same as above but coming **left** to pass.

One Prolonged-One Short-One Prolonged-One Short - An agreement signal given by **stand-on** vessel in a narrow channel to vessel desiring to pass. ‡

INLAND

HEAD ON

One Short Blast - I **INTEND** to leave you on my port side. Both craft must give this same signal **before** the maneuver.

Two Short Blasts - I **INTEND** to leave you on my starboard side. Both vessels signal **before** the maneuver.

Three Short Blasts - I am operating astern propulsion.

CROSSING

One Short Blast - Same as International except for one important difference. The signal is **returned** by the stand-on craft **BEFORE** the give-way craft can complete the maneuver.

OVERTAKING

One Short Blast - Same as International except the vessel ahead returns the signal indicating agreement for the maneuver.

Two Short Blasts - Same as International except the vessel ahead returns the signal indicating agreement for the maneuver.

There are no special "Narrow Channel" overtaking signals in Inland waters. ‡

In both International and Inland Rules, a short blast has the duration of about 1 second. A prolonged blast runs between four and six seconds. They are called whistle signals. These signals change when the fog comes in. See page 103.

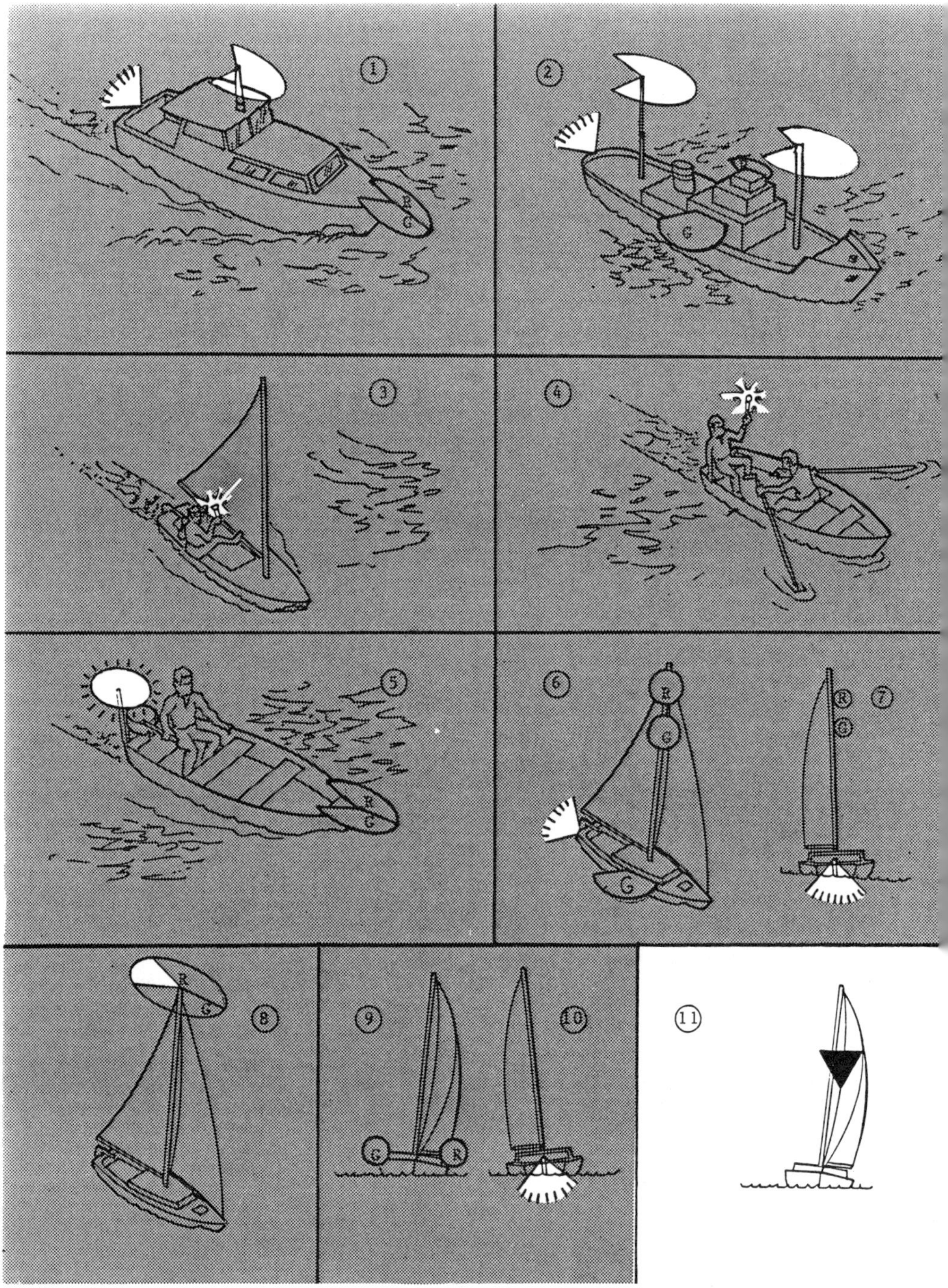
1
R
G
2
G
3
4
5
R
G
6
R
G
G
7
R
G
8
R
G
9
G
R
10
11

1) **INTERNATIONAL** - Power vessel less than 50 meters in length. Needs one 225° masthead light foreward. If less than 12 meters **may** exhibit an all-round (360°) white light & sidelights. **All** sternlights are 135° of arc.

INLAND - If less than 12 meters can use 360° light in lieu of masthead light, (See #5 below) and combined sidelights can be used.

3) **INTERNATIONAL** - If less than 7 meters in length sailboats can use electric torch (flashlight) or lantern to show in time to prevent collision...if sidelights are impractical.

INLAND - Same.

5) **INTERNATIONAL** - If less than 7 meters and making less than 7 knots the 360° light aft can be used in lieu of the masthead light forward. Sidelights to be used if practicable. If less than 12 meters, the 360° light can be used, but the combined sidelights **must be** used.

INLAND - If less than **12 meters** the 360° light can be used in lieu of the masthead lights. The sidelights **must be** used.

8) **INTERNATIONAL** - A Special arrangement for running lights on sailboats less than 20 meters in length.

INLAND - Same.

2) **INTERNATIONAL** - Example of power vessel 50 meters or greater in length. The after masthead light is added and must be higher than the one forward. Both are 225° arcs. Due to length, sidelights are now split and the usual sternlight is required. The after masthead light is optional for vessels less than 50 meters in length.

INLAND - Almost the same. On the Great Lakes, any craft can opt for a 360° light aft to replace the after masthead light and sternlight.

4) **INTERNATIONAL** - Rowboats can light up like sailboats. The white "lantern" (flashlight) is required when sidelights are not available or impractical. Collision prevention is the whole key. Or, as Thucydides put it: "A collision at sea can ruin your entire day."

INLAND - Same.

6) & 7) **INTERNATIONAL** - Sailboats *less than 20 meters* have a special option. They can exhibit 360° red over green lights at the masthead. When this option is used the combined sidelights and sternlight mast-top combination shown in #8 cannot be used.

INLAND - Same.

9) A sailboat shown head-on. Note that no white light can be seen. **Number 10** is the sternview showing the required 135° sternlight. This is the case both **International** and **Inland.**

11) **INTERNATIONAL** - Dayshape for sailboat with sails up but also with engine running. She is no longer considered a sailboat, but a power vessel.

INLAND - Not required on sailboats under sail with engines running if less than 12 meters in length.

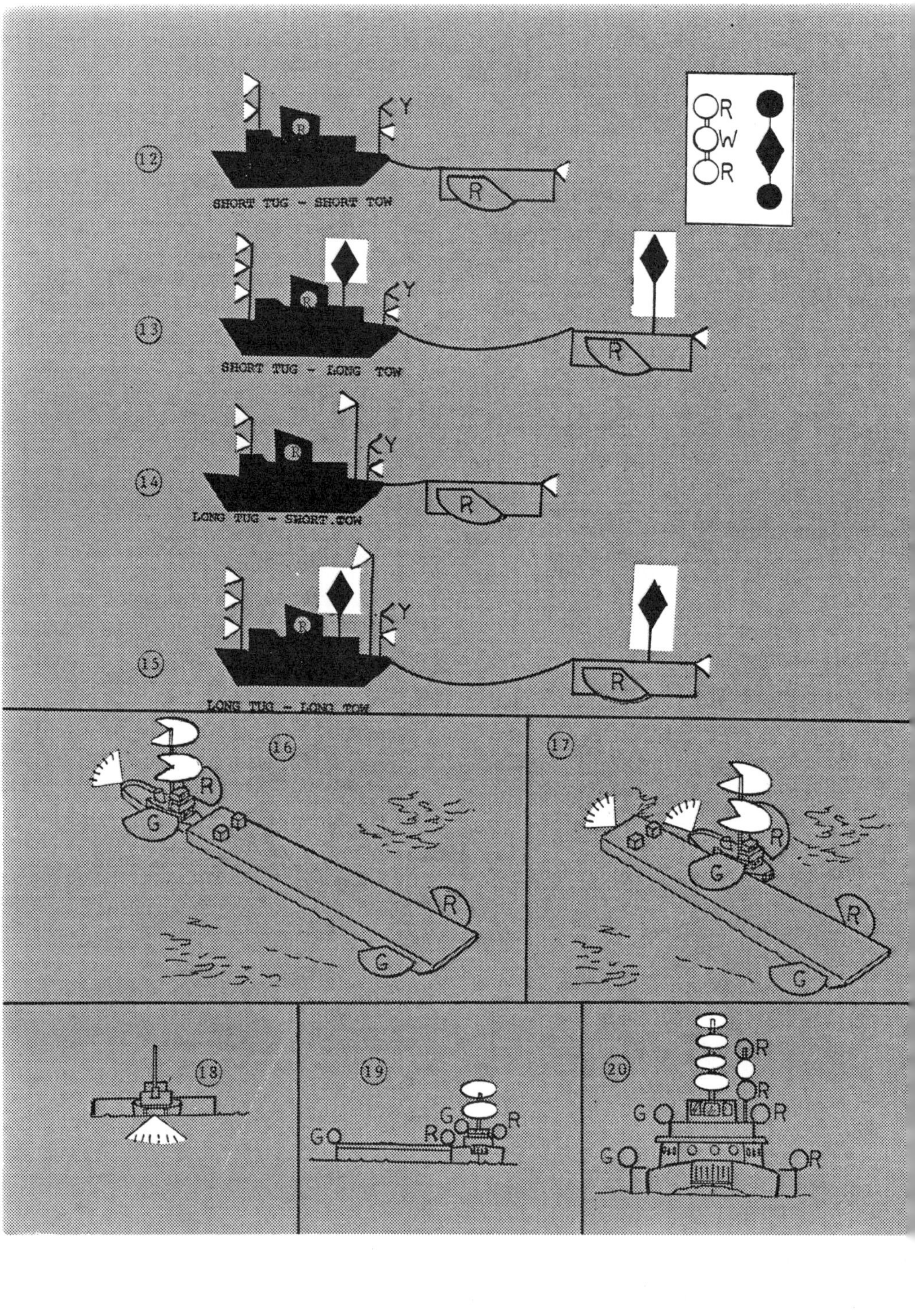

12
SHORT TUG - SHORT TOW
13
SHORT TUG - LONG TOW
14
LONG TUG - SHORT TOW
15
LONG TUG - LONG TOW
16
17
18
19
20

INTERNATIONAL TUGS

Develop this memory crutch for the International Tugs:

If the tug is less than 50 meters in length it's a "short tug".

If the tug is 50 meters or greater in length it's a "long tug".

NOW THE BARGES THEY ARE TOWING BEHIND.

If the barge is less than 200 meters astern it's a "short tow".

If the barge is 200 meters or farther, it's a "long tow".

Now read the next column on your right.

COMPARE THE DESCRIPTIONS BELOW WITH THE TUGS ON THE FACING PAGE

12) Short tug-short tow. Two 225° masthead lights forward.

13) Short tug-long tow. Three 225° masthead lights forward. The diamond dayshape for the daytime and located as far forward as possible.

14) Long tug-short tow. Same as #12 above but add a 225° after masthead light. Thus, viewed head-on you would see three white lights coming right at you.

15) Long tug-long tow. Same as #13 above but add a 225° after masthead light. And don't forget the diamond dayshape. **It's only needed when the tow is more than 200 meters astern** both here and in #13 above. Required on both tug and tow.

Did you notice the sternlights? Yellow over white. Both 135° arc. But careful here. The yellow one is called a "**towing** light", but the white is still a "**stern**light".

16) This is a short tug pushing her barge. Note the yellow towing light is eliminated-she is not "towing", she's "pushing". This is the one rare occasion when the barge does not need a sternlight. Note that tug and barges **ALWAYS** need sidelights. All vessels or barges towed behind or alongside always need stern & sidelights. In #16, if the tug were a "long tug" she would need an after masthead light.

18) Tug pushing her tow as seen from astern. No yellow towing light necessary.

17) Short tug with her barge alongside. Note that now sternlight is required on barge.

19) Short tug with barge alongside.

20) Long tug with her barge and coming right at you! Also note the dayshape for "restricted in ability to maneuver". The barge's sidelights should be visible on each side of the tug.

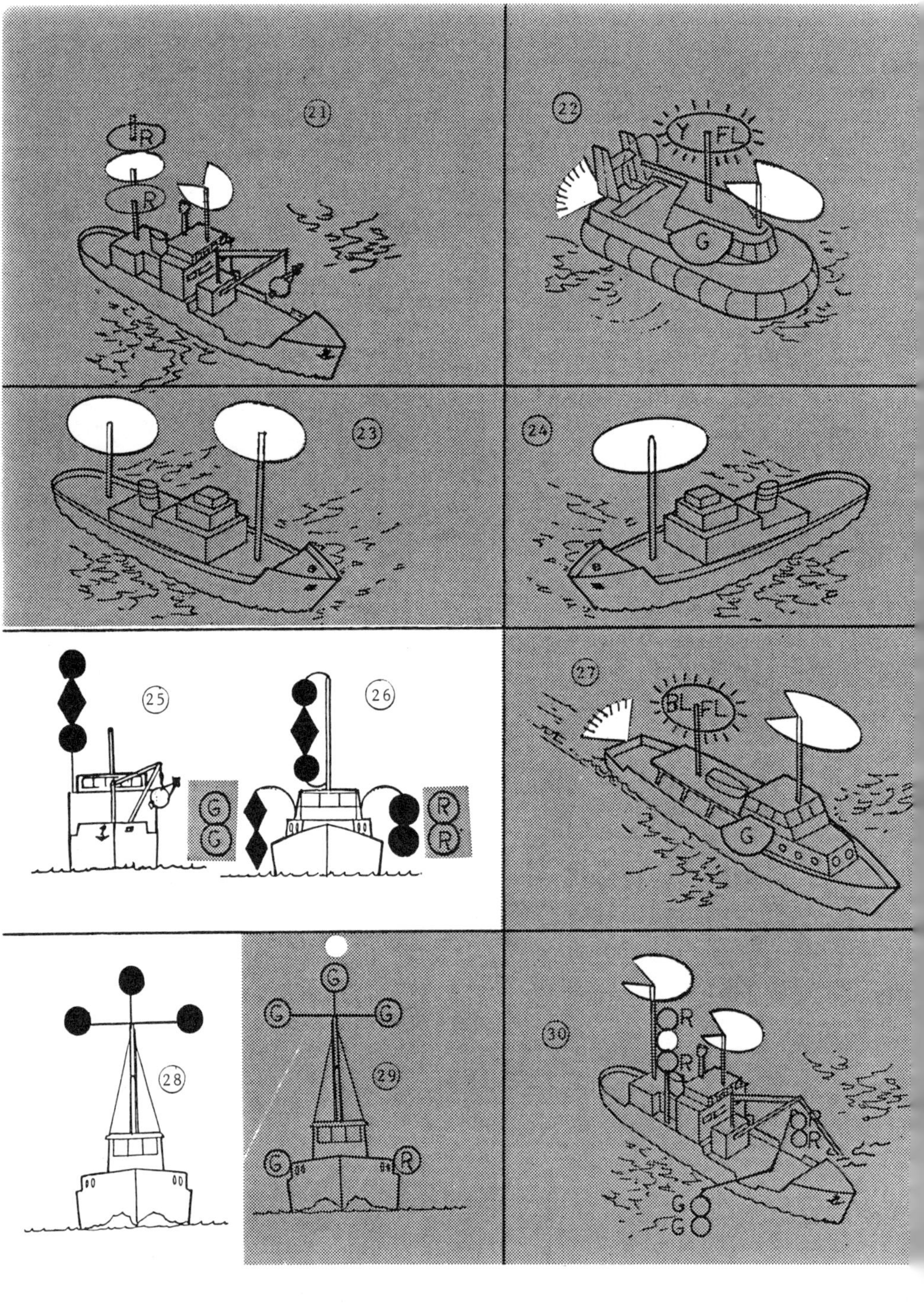

21
R
R
22
Y FL
G
23
24
25
G
G
26
R
R
27
BL FL
G
28
29
G
G
G
G
R
30
R
R
R
R
G
G

21) **INTERNATIONAL** - Coast Guard Buoy Tender. The 360° vertically arranged red-white-red -offset from centerline- indicates restricted in ability to maneuver. Since the vessel is not actually making way the sidelights are extinguished. Anchor lights are not required as technically, she is not anchored.

INLAND - Same.

23) **INTERNATIONAL** - Vessel 50 meters or more in length and at anchor. Note that both lights are 360°, **atop** masts and are reversed in position from those viewed on a vessel underway. Not like masthead lights which are lower than tips of masts. The stern anchor light is LOWER than the forward one. Vessels 100 meters or more in length must **also** illuminate their decks at night. Black ball is the dayshape for being at anchor. All dayhapes are black, except flags.

INLAND - Same.

25 & 26) **INTERNATIONAL** - Number 25 is the dayshape for a vessel restricted in her ability to maneuver.
Number 26 is engaged in some form of underwater work. Passing side is denoted by the black diamonds over the side. The night counterpart is #30 below. Note: Underwater work is anything from telephone cable to having a hardhat diver down.

INLAND - Same, except vessels less than 12 meters need not signal unless diving operations are in progress.

28 & 29) **INTERNATIONAL** - Minesweeper. Considered restricted in ability to maneuver without having to use the signal. The three black balls or three green lights are reserved for minesweepers only. You must stay clear of the vessel by 1,000 meters.

INLAND - Same, except stay clear of sides 500 meters, stern by 1,000 meters.

22) **INTERNATIONAL** - A "non-displacement" craft. Here, a hovercraft. Needs all the usual lights PLUS a "flashing light". A flashing light on a vessel is one which always flashes at 120 fpm.

INLAND -Same.

24) **INTERNATIONAL** - Vessel less than 50 meters in length and at anchor. Only one 360° white light required. Vessels less than 7 meters in length need not show the light if not anchored in area normally used by other vessels.

INLAND - Same except vessels less than 20 meters are exempt in approved anchorage areas.

27) **INTERNATIONAL** - No special law enforcement lights are indicated under International Rules of The Road.

INLAND - Flashing Blue Light. Law enforcement. Federal or local.

30) **INTERNATIONAL** - Underwater operation. For example, dredging. Favorite on CG exams. Red 360° lights mark the non-passing side. Stay away. Pass on the green light side. Excusing the perspective of the sketch, these lights are always higher than the sidelights.

Note absence of side and sternlights. He is not making way. "Underway" is defined as not at anchor, not aground and/or not tied to a pier or dock.

INLAND - Same.

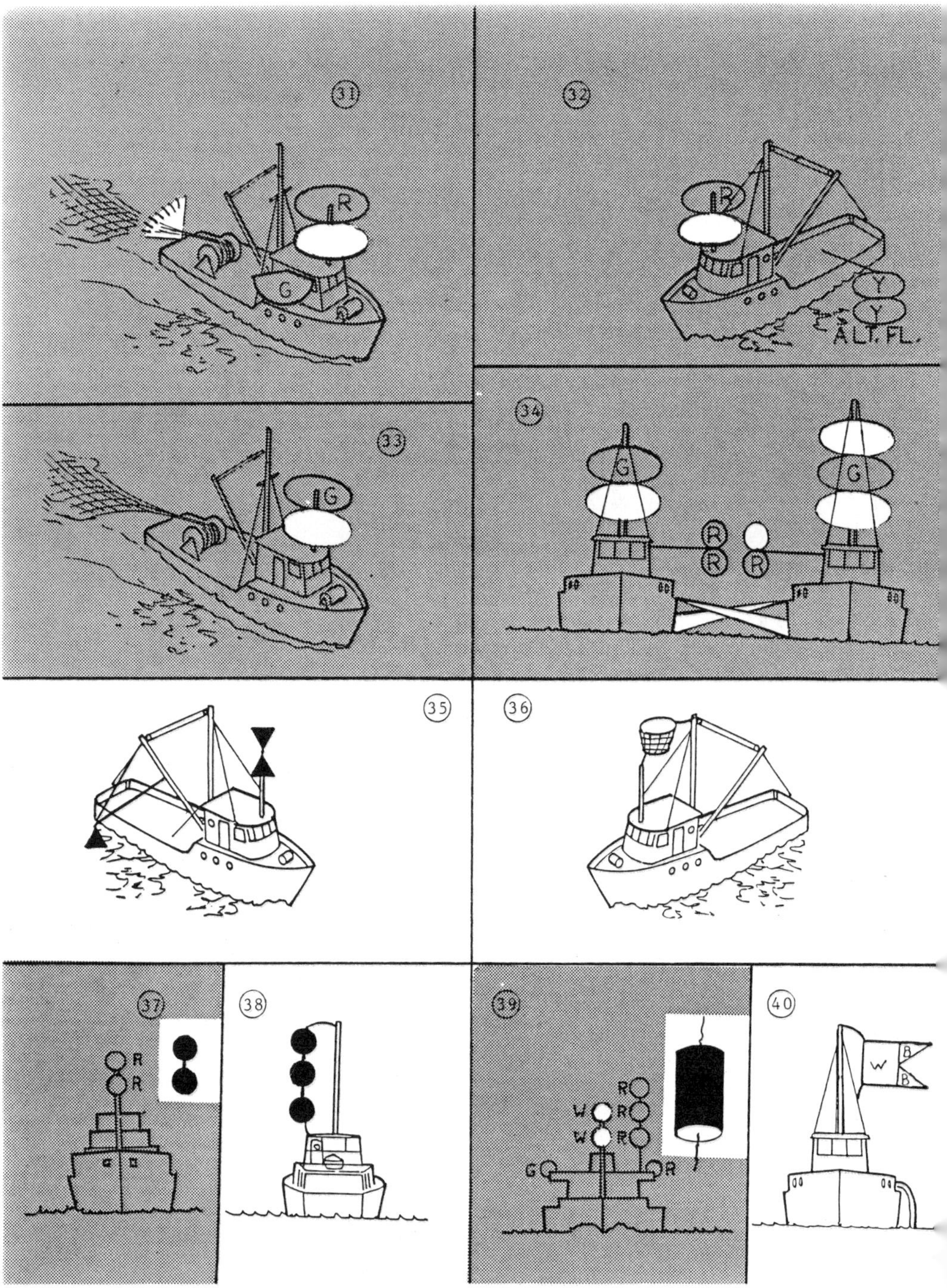
31
R
G
32
R
Y
Y
ALT. FL.
33
G
34
G
G
R
R
R
35
36
37
R
R
38
39
R
W
R
W
R
G
R
40
W
B
B

31) **INTERNATIONAL** - A fishing vessel is considered fishing only when using lines, nets or trawls. Trolling is not considered fishing! "Red-over-white, Fishing Tonight." Side and sternlights displayed only when underway. Special lights and dayshapes for fishing shown only when actually engaged in fishing. Fishing in navigable channels or fairways is illegal.

INLAND - Same.

33) **INTERNATIONAL** - A trawler has different lights than the other fishing vessels. Green over white. Frequent test question. Trawling means she is dragging the bottom as opposed to the fishing vessel above with nets or lines. The net shown here is weighted and on the way to the bottom.

INLAND - Same.

35) **INTERNATIONAL** - Dayshapes for fishing vessels. Two cones apex to apex and up high. Small cone over side -should be higher than sidelights- indicates nets on that side horizontally out 150 meters or more. At night this is a white 360° light in the direction of the gear. Cone over side is NOT used by trawlers...nor is the 360° light.

INLAND -Same.

37 & 38) **INTERNATIONAL** - Not under command. Two red lights, each 360° arranged vertically. "red-over-red," the captain's dead." Engine down, prop fell off, drifting. If a vessel is aground this same signal is used but a white anchor light is added, or two if the vessel is 50 meters or greater in length. Three black balls is aground. Popular test question.

INLAND - Same.

32) **INTERNATIONAL** - Purse seiners can show a special signal of two 360° vertically arranged flashing yellow lights when hampered by their fishing gear. They flash alternately every second.

INLAND - Same.

34) **INTERNATIONAL** - Special lights for trawlers when fishing in fleet or as a team. They can shine searchlights on each other's hull. Separate signals to indicate current maneuver: Vertically arrange two white lights=shooting the nets; white-over-red=pulling the nets; red-over-red=nets hung up on obstruction below. Special masthead lights green over white. If less than 50 meters in length the top white masthead light is optional. Only when actually underway would the sidelights and sternlight be lighted.

INLAND - Same.

36) **INTERNATIONAL** - The only standard dayshape not black is the basket for fishing vessels less than 20 meters in length. The two cones in #35 can be used instead.

INLAND - Same.

39) **INTERNATIONAL** - The cylinder shape describes a deep draft vessel in a shallow channel. Cargo vessels, freighters or very large craft unable to deviate from course. At night, three vertically arranged 360° red lights.

INLAND - At this writing, no such signal inland. However, no vessel may restrict the passage of another craft which is in a traffic zone by crossing the zone or fairway.

40) **SPECIAL NOTE: - The Alfa Flag** is for divers down. Rigid construction to show all around.

41
Y
Y
R
G
R
G
42
Y
Y
R
G
Y
FL
R
G
43
R
R
G
44
R
R
R
G
45
R
Y
R
G
G
46
R
G
R
47
Y
R
G
48
R
Y Y Y Y R
R
R Y Y

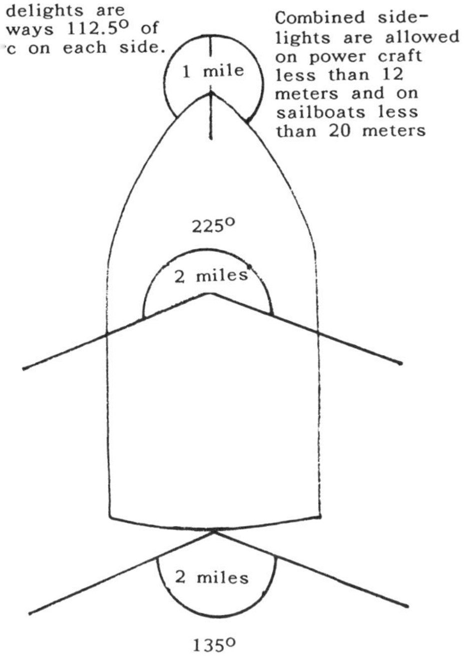

VESSEL LESS THAN 12 METERS

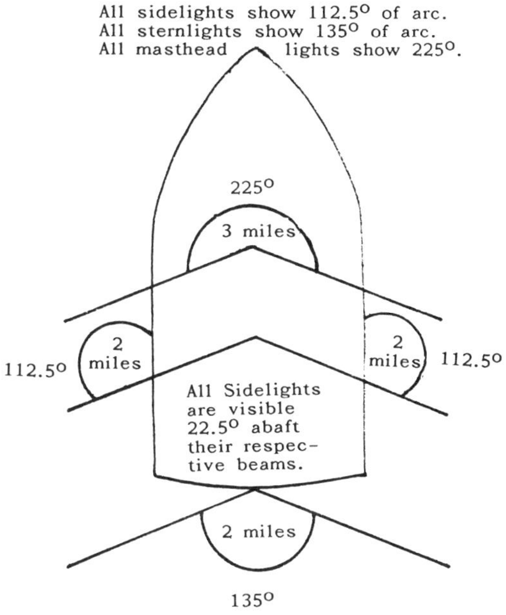

VESSEL GREATER THAN 12 METERS
BUT LESS THAN 20 METERS

VESSEL 20 METERS OR GREATER
BUT LESS THAN 50 METERS

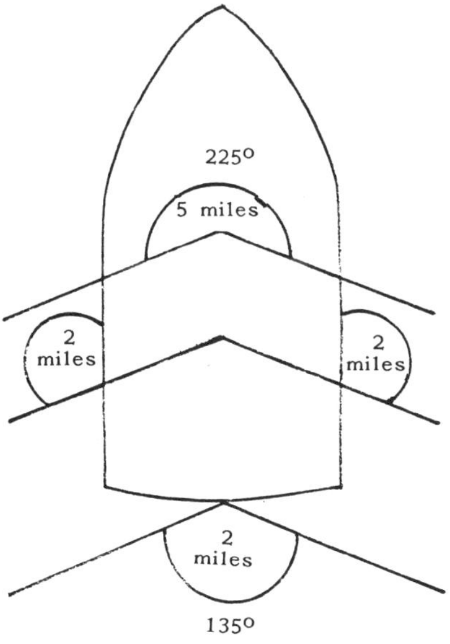

VESSEL 50 METERS OR GREATER
IN LENGTH.

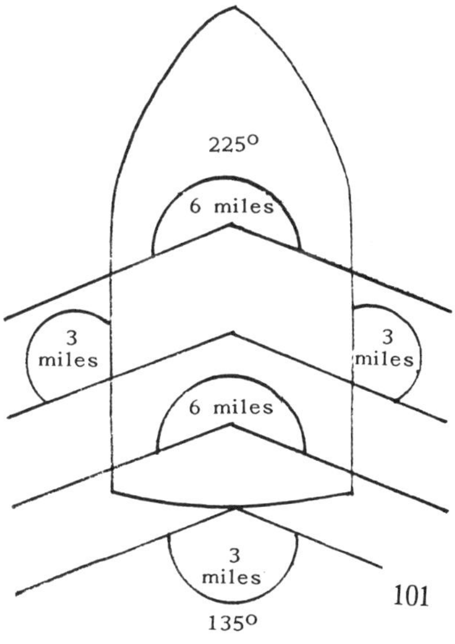

☆ THE INTERNATIONAL PECKING ORDER ☆

Below, in matching columns, is a simplified version of the so-called "pecking order". The farther down the pole the less right-of-way is conferred. Top man is Not Under Command. The Unified rules (read Inland) and International are very much alike with one glaring exception in #3. However, the Unified rules are very clear as regards craft travelling in traffic patterns or rivers, fairways and channels. Note: the lights below are "all-round" lights visible for 360°.

VESSEL

1) Not Under Command: No steerage , no power or perhaps underway with no way on. "Red over red, the captain's dead."

2) Restricted In Ability To Maneuver: Underwater operations, surveying, fueling at sea, recovering aircraft, transferring cargo, fuel or personnel, servicing aids to navigation, dredging.

Towing-severely restricted in maneuverability. Note: this requires TWO separate signals; one indicating towing, + restricted maneuverability.

Minesweeper. No other restricted in ability signal required, but needs masthead light(s).

3) Vessel Constrained By Draft: A deep draft vessel in a narrow or shallow channel. No such signal Inland.

4) Fishing or Trawling: Fishing is using "lines, nets or trawls" but NOT trolling. Note separate signals for "fishing" vs. "trawling".

5) Sailing: Sailboat under sail. Red over green masthead lights optional. Sailboats must display inverted cone when under sail with engines running.

6) Powerboats: Low end of totem pole. Only lights required are those specified in regular rules section on lights and dayshapes. Note that towing is included here unless the skipper indicates otherwise by hoisting signals indicated in #2 above. ‡

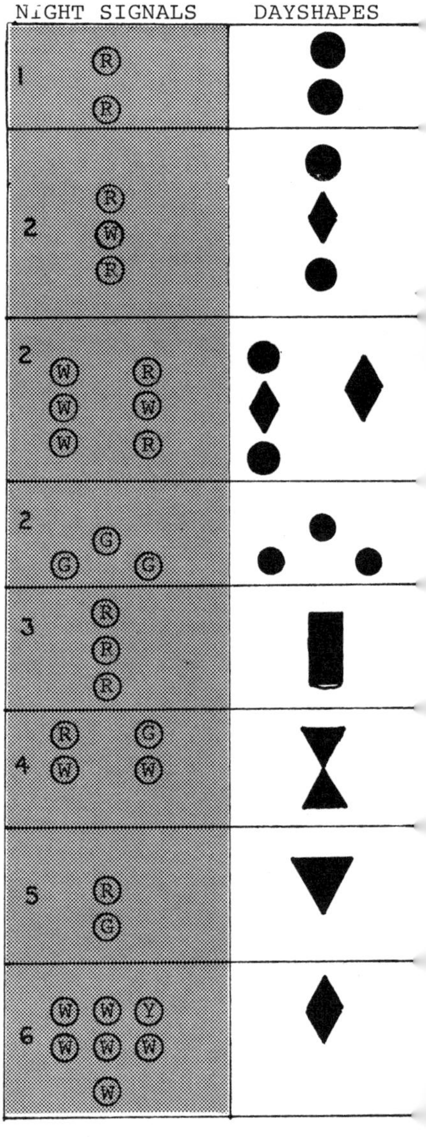

RESTRICTED VISIBILITY

SIGNALS WHICH ARE GIVEN AT LEAST ONCE EVERY TWO MINUTES BY VESSELS UNDERWAY.

One Prolonged Blast - Given by vessels underway "in or near" any area in which the visibility is restricted for any reason or in any way.

Two Prolonged Blasts - Underway, but stopped. No way on.

One Prolonged - Two Shorts - To be given **INLAND** in restricted visibility underway **or** at **anchor** by:
Fishing vessels fishing, or any craft restricted in ability to maneuver.
The same signal is also given **only** when underway by sailboats, vessels not under command and tugs pushing or towing. See flashcards and read p.49.

In **International** waters one prolonged and two shorts are sounded by any craft underway **or** at anchor when fishing or working vessels restricted in ability to maneuver. Also to be given by craft underway when: constrained by draft, restricted in ability to maneuver, not under command, sailboats, tugs pushing or towing and fishing vessels when fishing.

One Prolonged - Three Short - Signal to be given by any vessel when being towed IF MANNED; if more than one vessel, then the last vessel in tow sounds off, but only if MANNED.

Four Short Blasts - Identity signal for a pilot vessel. Pilot vessel must also give one prolonged blast when underway, and any other signals for a vessel of their respective size. ‡

SIGNALS WHICH ARE GIVEN AT LEAST ONCE EVERY MINUTE BY VESSELS ANCHORED OR AGROUND

One Short-One Prolonged-One Short Given by a vessel at anchor. This is an optional signal to give extra warning of one's position.

Five Second Ringing Of A Bell - Given by vessels at anchor. In Inland waters some vessels do not need to give this signal if anchored in special designated anchorage areas. This includes vessels less than 20 meters in length, barges, canal boats and scows plus other "non-descript" craft.

Five Second Bell - followed by - **Five Second Gong in Stern Area.** Given by vessels at anchor of 100 meters or more in length.

Three Distinct Strokes on the Bell followed by - **Five Second Ringing of the Bell** - followed by - **Three More Strokes on the Bell** - is the signal for a vessel aground. And if you think that's funny; if the vessel is 100 meters or more in length, the above signal must be followed by a **Five Second Ringing of the Gong** in the stern area.

VESSELS LESS THAN 12 METERS IN LENGTH: Not required to give the above bell signals but must have ready at hand some sound producing signal. ‡

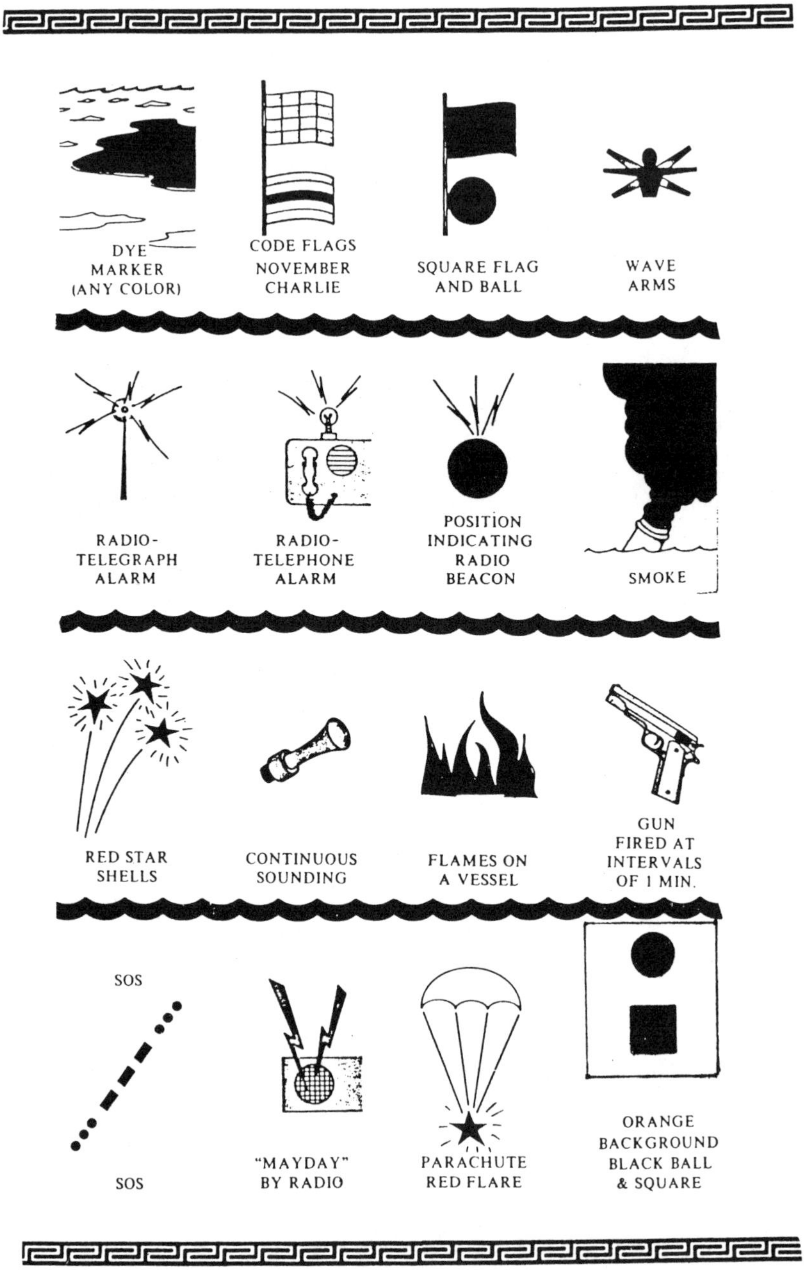
DYE MARKER (ANY COLOR)
CODE FLAGS NOVEMBER CHARLIE
SQUARE FLAG AND BALL
WAVE ARMS
RADIO-TELEGRAPH ALARM
RADIO-TELEPHONE ALARM
POSITION INDICATING RADIO BEACON
SMOKE
RED STAR SHELLS
CONTINUOUS SOUNDING
FLAMES ON A VESSEL
GUN FIRED AT INTERVALS OF 1 MIN.
SOS
SOS
"MAYDAY" BY RADIO
PARACHUTE RED FLARE
ORANGE BACKGROUND BLACK BALL & SQUARE

THE INLAND RULES

INLAND

PART A - GENERAL

RULE #1

Application

(a) These rules apply to all vessels upon the inland waters of the United States, and to vessels of the United States on the Canadian waters of the Great Lakes to the extent that there is no conflict with Canadian law.

(b)(i) These Rules constitute special rules made by an appropriate authority within the meaning of **Rule 1(b)** of the International Regulations.

(ii) All vessels complying with the construction and equipment requirements of the International Regulations are considered to be in compliance with these Rules.

(c) Nothing in these Rules shall interfere with the operation of any special rules made by the Secretary of the Navy with respect to additional station or signal lights and shapes or whistle signals for ships of war and vessels proceeding under convoy, or by the Secretary with respect to additional station or signal lights and shapes for fishing vessels engaged in fishing as a fleet. These additional station or signal lights and shapes or whistle signals shall, so far as possible, be such that they cannot be mistaken for any light, shape, or signal authorized elsewhere under these Rules. Notice of such special rules shall be published in the Federal Register and, after the effective date specified in such notice, they shall have effect as if they were a part of these Rules.

(d) Vessel traffic service regulations may be in effect in certain areas.

(Cont'd)

INLAND RULE #1 - COMMENTS

Rules #1 Inland is essentially an Inland version of the corresponding International Rule.

1a) The Great Lakes are added.

1c) The US is agreeing to abide as closely as possible, but the Secretary (meaning the Secretary of the Navy) may change a few things occasionally.

1d) Here's the **most important deviation** from the International Rule #1, yet it's the most brief. Essentially, there are times when the ordinary rules of keeping right, pass to port, hug the channel bank and other commonly accepted practices must be temporarily amended. In the US this is called "Vessel Traffic Systems," (VTS) and is set up on a local basis. See Inland Rule #10. For example, on the Western Rivers, (the Mississippi and its tribs) there are places where staying to the far right will put you aground and not always may the man running downstream with a following current justify the right-of-way. In Marina del Rey out in California, the center of the ingress-egress channel is reserved for tacking sailboats. Power craft are restricted to narrow channels on each side of this wider center channel, thus lessening the chances of collision.

If you are out there someplace bobbing around how do you learn of these special deviations? The answer is: Don't go until you've read the charts and examined closely the local cruising guides. It's the old U.S. Power Squadron motto: "Know Before You Go," and applies in many varied sea related cautions.

RULE #1 (Cont'd)

(e) *Whenever the Secretary shall have determined that a vessel of special construction or purpose cannot comply fully with the provisions of any of these Rules with respect to the number, position, range or arc of visibility of lights or shapes, as well as to the disposition and characteristics of sound-signalling appliances such vessel shall comply with such other provisions in regard to number, position, range or arc of visibility of lights or signalling appliances, as her Government shall have determined to be the closest possible compliance with these Rules in respect to that vessel.*

(f) The Secretary may accept a certificate of alternative compliance issued by a contracting party to the International Regulations if he determines that the alternative compliance standards of the contracting party are substantially the same as those of the United States.

RULE #2

Responsibility

(a) Nothing in these Rules shall exonerate any vessel, or the owner, master or crew thereof, from the consequences of any neglect to comply with these Rules or of the neglect of any precaution which may be required by the ordinary practice of seamen, or by the special circumstances of the case.

(b) In construing and complying with these Rules due regard shall be had to all dangers of navigation and collision and to any special circumstances, including the limitations of the vessels involved, which may make a departure from these Rules necessary to avoid immediate danger.

INLAND RULE #2 - COMMENTS

Note italics on facing page. See page 11.

See comments on International Rule 2. They are essentially the same as the Inland counterpart.

RULE #3

General Definitions

For the purpose of these Rules and this Act, except where the context otherwise requires:

(a) The word "vessel" includes every description of water craft, including nondisplacement craft and seaplanes, used or capable of being used as a means of transportation on water.

(b) The term "power-driven vessel" means any vessel propelled by machinery.

(c) The term "sailing vessel" means any vessel under sail provided that propelling machinery, if fitted, is not being used.

(d) The term "vessel engaged in fishing" means any vessel fishing with nets, lines, trawls or other fishing apparatus which restricts maneuverability, but does not include a vessel fishing with trolling lines or other fishing apparatus which do not restrict maneuverability.

(e) The word "seaplane" includes any aircraft designed to maneuver on the water.

(f) The term "vessel not under command" means a vessel which through some exceptional circumstance is unable to keep out of the way of another vessel.

(g) The term "vessel restricted in her ability to maneuver" means a vessel which from the nature of her work is restricted in her ability to maneuver as required by these Rules and is therefore unable to keep out of the way of another vessel. The term 'vessels restricted in their ability to maneuver' shall include but not be limited to:

(i) a vessel engaged in laying, servicing or picking up a navigation mark, submarine cable or pipeline;

(ii) a vessel engaged in dredging, surveying or underwater operations;

(Cont'd)

INLAND RULE #3 - COMMENTS

Add to those International comments on this Rule the fact that the term "underway" should be clearly understood.

1h) A vessel can be underway, yet with no way on. Sitting still. Drifting. While this may not seem noteworthy, the subtle difference is important when dealing with various night signals (lights) on some working vessels. Most notable is the fishing vessel and is the basic subject area for many Coast Guard license exam questions. See comments under Rule 26.

CG license aspirants stand advised that International Rule 3(h) italics change is not to be included here. Inland does not recognize "vessels constrained by draft."

Note that vessels "Restricted in their ability to maneuver" are wide and varied. Even the term under 3(g) states "...but not limited to." Also, these are generally considered to be working vessels as opposed to, say, a becalmed sailboat. They are buoy tenders, tugs with tows, aircraft carriers and yes, even minesweepers. Of course, if it's a working minesweeper, what are you doing out there in the first place?

And what makes a vessel "restricted in ability to maneuver?" Answer: The captain's discretion. He can hoist the appropriate signals at his own whim. We will revisit this favorite test subject again under Rule 18 and the nitty things related thereto.

(Cont'd)

Rule #3 (Cont'd)

(g)(iii) a vessel engaged in replenishment or transferring persons, provisions or cargo while underway;

(iv) a vessel engaged in the launching or recovery of aircraft;

(v) A vessel engaged in minesweeping operations; and

(vi) a vessel engaged in a towing operation such as severely restricts the towing vessel and her tow in their ability to deviate from their course.

(h) The word "underway" means that a vessel is not at anchor, or made fast to the shore, or aground.

(i) The words "length" and "breadth" of a vessel mean her length overall and greatest breadth.

(j) Vessels shall be deemed to be in sight of one another only when one can be observed visually from the other.

(k) The term "restricted visibility" means any condition in which visibility is restricted by fog, mist, falling snow, heavy rainstorms, sandstorms, or any other similar causes.

(l) "Western Rivers" means the Mississippi River, its tributaries, South Pass, and Southwest Pass, to the navigational demarcation lines of the United States, and the Port Allen-Morgan City Alternate Route, and that part of the Atchafalaya River above its junction with the Port Allen-Morgan City Alternate Route including the Old River and the Red River;

(m) "Great Lakes" means the Great Lakes and their connecting and tributary waters including the Calumet River as far as the Thomas J, O'Brien Lock and Controlling Works (between mile 326 and 327), the Chicago River as far as the east side of the Ashland Avenue Bridge (between mile 321 and 322), and the Saint Lawrence River as far east as the lower exit of Saint Lambert Lock;

(Cont'd)

INLAND RULE #3 - COMMENTS

The chart section below comes from the TR 1210 (training chart) and shows an example of a COLREGS demarcation line as per Rules 3(o) on page 114. It is rather typical of **most** demarcation lines in that it connects to two prominent landmarks. This particular one indicates the Inland of Buzzards Bay in Massachuetts.

It is not to be used for navigation.

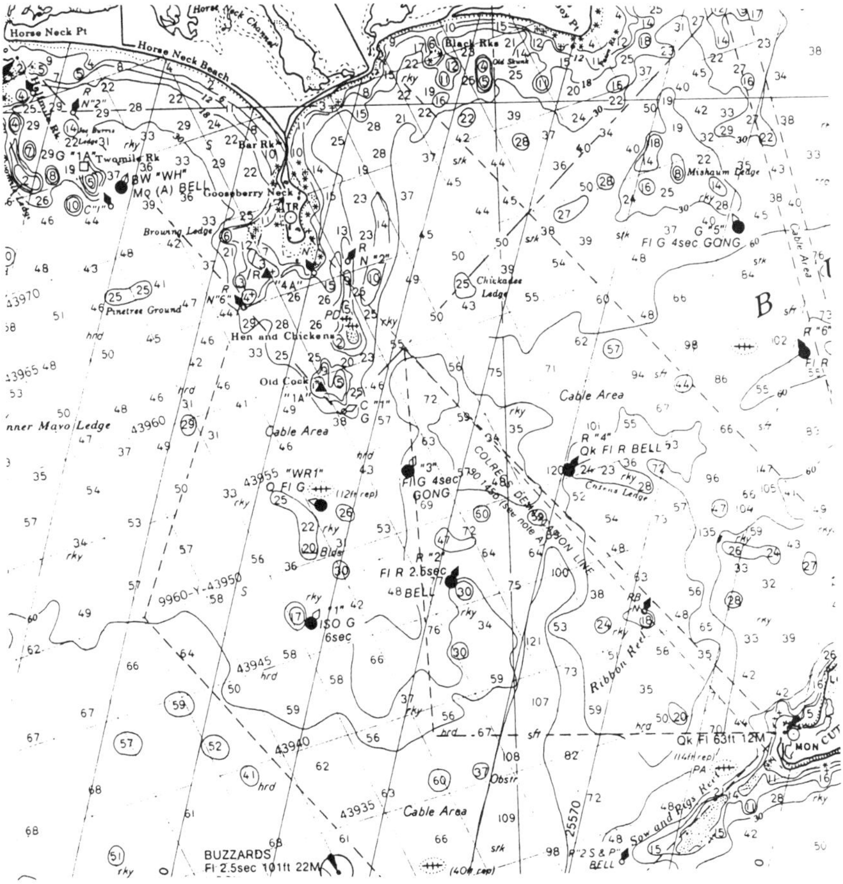

RULE #3 (Cont'd)

(n) "Secretary" means the Secretary of the department in which the Coast Guard is operating;

(o) "Inland Waters" means the navigable waters of the United States shoreward of the navigational demarcation lines dividing the high seas from harbors, rivers, and other inland waters of the United States and the waters of the Great Lakes on the United States side of the International Boundary;

(p) "Inland Rules" or "Rules" mean the Inland Navigational Rules and the annexes thereto, which govern the conduct of vessels and specify the lights, shapes, and sound signals that apply on inland waters; and

(q) "International Regulations" means the International Regulations for Preventing Collisions at Sea, 1972, including annexes currently in force for the United States.

INLAND RULE #3 - COMMENTS

(Cont'd)

For definitions and where to find them regarding "Inland" waters, see page 12.

Annexes are addenda made to both International and Inland Rules. They are found in the back of this volume. Four annexes for the International Rules and five for Inland Rules.

Basically, these Annexes deal with the more technical aspects of lights and sound producing apparatus. For the most part, Coast Guard license candidates need not be concerned with all of them. Instead, concentrate on the special lights for fishing vessels found in Annex II, the Distress Signals as outlined in Annex IV, and the **Inland** Annex V, (Pilot Rules) paragraph 88.13 (a-c) wherein the nature and anchoring of barges is discussed.

PART B

STEERING AND SAILING RULES

Subpart I-Conduct of Vessels in Any Condition of Visibility.

Rule #4

Application

Rules in this Subpart apply in any condition of visibility.

RULE #5

Look-out

Every vessel shall at all times maintain a proper look-out by sight and hearing as well as by all available means appropriate in the prevailing circumstances and conditions so as to make a full appraisal of the situation and of the risk of collision.

INLAND RULES #4 AND #5 - COMMENTS

International and Inland Rules 4 and 5 are identical. Please see Comments under International Rules 4 and 5.

RULE #6

Safe Speed

Every vessel shall at all times proceed at a safe speed so that she can take proper and effective action to avoid collision and be stopped within a distance appropriate to the prevailing circumstances and conditions.

In determining a safe speed the following factors shall be among those taken into account:

(a) By all vessels;
(i) the state of visibility;
(ii) the traffic including concentrations of fishing vessels or any other vessels;
(iii) the maneuverability of the vessel with special reference to stopping distance and turning ability in the prevailing conditions;
(iv) at night the presence of background light such as from shore lights or from back scatter of her own lights.
(v) the state of wind, sea and current, and the proximity of navigational hazards;
(vi) the draft in relation to the available depth of water;

(b) Additionally, by vessels with operational radar:
(i) the characteristics, efficiency and limitations of the radar equipment;
(ii) any contraints imposed by the radar range scale in use;
(iii) the effect on radar detection of the sea state, weather and other sources of interference;
(iv) the possibility that small vessels, ice and other floating objects may not be detected by radar at an adequate range;
(v) the number, location and movement of vessels detected by radar;
(vi) the more exact assessment of the visibility that may be possible when radar is used to determine the range of vessels or other objects in the vicinity.

INLAND RULE #6 - COMMENTS

International and Inland Rule #6 are identical. Please see Comments under the Interntional Rule #6

RULE #7

Risk of Collision

(a) Every vessel shall use all available means appropriate to the prevailing circumstances and conditions to determine if risk of collision exists. If there is any doubt such risk shall be deemed to exist.

(b) Proper use shall be made of radar equipment if fitted and operational, including long-range scanning to obtain early warning of risk of collision and radar plotting or equivalent systematic observation of detected objects.

(c) Assumptions shall not be made on the basis of scanty information, especially scanty radar information.

(d) In determining if risk of collision exists the following considerations shall be among those taken into account:

(i) such risk shall be deemed to exist if the compass bearing of an approaching vessel does not appreciably change.

(ii) such risk may sometimes exist even when an appreciable bearing change is evident, particularly when approaching a very large vessel or a tow or when approaching a vessel at close range.

INLAND RULE #7 - COMMENTS

International and Inland Rules #7 are identical. Please see Comments under Inland Rule #7

RULE #8

Action to Avoid Collision

(a) Any action taken to avoid collision shall, if the circumstances of the case admit, be positive, made in ample time and with due regard to the observance of good seamanship.

(b) Any alteration of course and/or speed to avoid collision shall, if the circumstances of the case admit, be large enough to be readily apparent to another vessel observing visually or by radar; a succession of small alterations of course and/or speed should be avoided.

(c) If there is sufficient sea room, alteration of course alone may be the most effective action to avoid a close-quarters situation provided that it is made in good time, is substantial and does not result in another close-quarters situation.

(d) Action taken to avoid collision with another vessel shall be such as to result in passing at a safe distance. The effectiveness of the action shall be carefully checked until the other vessel is finally past and clear.

(e) If necessary to avoid collision or allow more time to assess the situation, a vessel shall slacken her speed or take all way off by stopping or reversing her means of propulsion.

(f)(i) *A vessel which, by any of these rules, is required not to impede the passage or safe passage of another vessel shall, when required by the circumstances of the case, take early action to allow sufficient sea room for the safe passage of the other vessel.*

(f)(ii) *A vessel required not to impede the passage or safe passage of another vessel is not relieved of this obligation if approaching the other vessel so as to involve the risk of collision and shall, when taking action, have full regard to the action which may be required by the rules of this part.*

(f)(iii) *A vessel the passage of which is not to be impeded remains fully obliged to comply with the rules of this part when the two vessels are approaching one another so as to involve risk of collision.*

INLAND RULE #8 - COMMENTS

With the exception of one word and a "/" in 8(b), both International and Inland Rules are identical. Please see Comments under Inland Rule #8.

For explanation of italics, please see page 11.

RULE #9

Narrow Channels

(a)(i) A vessel proceeding along a course of a narrow channel or fairway shall keep as near to the outer limit of the channel or fairway which lies on her starboard side as is safe and practicable.

(ii) Notwithstanding **paragraph (a)(i) and Rules 14(a)**, a power-driven vessel operating in narrow channels or fairways on the Great Lakes, Western Rivers, or waters specified by the Secretary, and proceeding downbound with a following current shall have the right-of-way over an upbound vessel, shall propose the manner and place of passage, and shall initiate the maneuvering signals prescribed by **Rules 34 (a)(i)**, as appropriate. The vessel proceeding upbound against the current shall hold as necessary to permit safe passing.

(b) A vessel of less than 20 meters in length or a sailing vessel shall not impede the passage of a vessel which can safely navigate only within a narrow channel or fairway.

(c) A vessel engaged in fishing shall not impede the passage of any other vessel navigating within a narrow channel or fairway.

(d) A vessel shall not cross a narrow channel or fairway if such crossing impedes the passage of a vessel which can safely navigate only within such channel or fairway. The latter vessel may use the sound signal prescribed in **Rule 34 (d)** if in doubt as to the intention of the crossing vessel.

(Cont'd)

INLAND RULE #9 - COMMENTS

International and Inland Rule 9 are almost identical with three notable differences.

1) The signals given for overtaking in narrow channels are different. Inland gives one signal, International gives an entirely different signal detailed in Rule 34.

2) There is an Inland Rule which gives the right-of-way to a downbound vessel **with a following current.** Look for the "downbound" reference in your Inland quiz question. If that word is not used, answer accordingly and file a protest asking if the question meant downbound, but didn't say so. Proves you're smart and should put you in the clear. With only thirty questions on the Rules test you need all the leeway you can get to make the required 90% score.

There is no such rule in International. Also note the Inland downbound vessel has the right-of-way, chooses the place of passing and **sounds the signal first.** In all other cases, the **give-way** vessel sounds the signals first.

3) Special note for Rule 9(d). Here, it says the danger signal **shall be** sounded. In International Rules it says the signal **can be** used. Nit-picky you say? Right! But, there are Rules questions on this very subject in both the International and Inland Rules exams. Thus, on the International test look for the multiple choice which indicates the signal is **optional.**

RULE #9 (Cont'd)

(e)(i) In a narrow channel or fairway when overtaking can take place only if the vessel to be overtaken has to take action to permit safe passing, the vessel intending to overtake shall indicate her intention by sounding the appropriate signal prescribed in **Rule 34 (c)(i).** The vessel to be overtaken shall, if in agreement, sound the appropriate signal prescribed in **Rule 34 (c)(ii)** and take steps to permit safe passing. If in doubt she may sound the signals prescribed in **Rule 34 (d).**

(ii) This Rule does not relieve the overtaking vessel of her obligation under **Rule 13.**

(f) A vessel nearing a bend or an area of a narrow channel or fairway where other vessels may be obscured by an intervening obstruction shall navigate with particular alertness and caution and shall sound the appropriate signal prescribed in **Rule 34(e).**

(g) Any vessel shall, if the circumstances of the case admit, avoid anchoring in a narrow channel.

RULE #10

Vessel Traffic Services

Each vessel required by regulation to participate in a vessel traffic service shall comply with the applicable regulations.

INLAND RULE #10 - COMMENTS

The cautious reader determined to conquer the Coast Guard Rules of The Road module would do well to note the contrast of the complexity between the International Rule #10 and the simplicity of the Inland Rule #10.

Keep in mind the Vessel Traffic Service (VTS) in the US is a complex one differing by the area in which one is navigating. One should acquire information well ahead regarding specific Rules in unfamiliar areas Inland. This is particularly true of the Western Rivers - i.e., rivers dumping into the Mississippi.

Please see Comment notes on Inland Rule 1d.

And again, there are no "inshore traffic zones" in U.S. waters.

SUBPART II-CONDUCT OF VESSELS IN SIGHT OF ONE ANOTHER

RULE #11

Application

Rules in this subpart apply to vessels in sight of one another.

RULE #12

Sailing Vessels

12(a) When two sailing vessels are approaching one another, so as to involve risk of collision, one of them shall keep out of the way of the other as follows:

12(a)(i) when each has the wind on a different side, the vessel which has the wind on the port side shall keep out of the way of the other;

12(a)(ii) when both have the wind on the same side, the vessel which is to windward shall keep out of the way of the vessel which is to leeward;

12(a)(iii) if a vessel with the wind on the port side sees a vessel to windward and cannot determine with certainty whether the other vessel has the wind on the port or on the starboard side, she shall keep out of the way of the other.

12(b) For the purposes of this Rule the windward side shall be deemed to be the side opposite to that on which the mainsail is carried or, in the case of a square-rigged vessel, the side opposite to that on which the largest fore-and-aft sail is carried.

INLAND RULE #11 - COMMENTS

International and Inland Rules 11 and 12 are identical with the exception of one insignificant word. Please see comments under International Rules 11-12.

RULE #13

Overtaking

(a) Notwithstanding anything contained in the **Rules 4 through 18**, any vessel overtaking any other shall keep out of the way of the vessel being overtaken.

(b) A vessel shall be deemed to be overtaking when coming up with another vessel from a direction more than 22.5 degrees abaft her beam, that is, in such a position with reference to the vessel she is overtaking, that at night she would be able to see only the sternlight of that vessel but neither of her sidelights.

(c) When a vessel is in any doubt as to whether she is overtaking another, she shall assume that this is the case and act accordingly.

(d) Any subsequent alteration of the bearing between the two vessels shall not make the overtaking vessel a crossing vessel within the meaning of these Rules or relieve her of the duty of keeping clear of the overtaken vessel until she is finally past and clear.

RULE #14

Head-On Situations

(a) When two power-driven vessels are meeting on reciprocal or nearly reciprocal courses so as to involve risk of collision each shall alter her course to starboard so that each shall pass on the portside of the other.

(b) Such a situation shall be deemed to exist when a vessel sees the other ahead or nearly ahead and by night she could see the masthead lights of the other in a line or nearly in a line or both sidelights and by day she observes the corresponding aspect of the other vessel.

(c) When a vessel is in any doubt as to whether such a situation exists she shall assume that it does exist and act accordingly.

INLAND RULES #13-14 - COMMENTS

International and Inland Rules are identical. Please see Comments for Rules 13 and 14 under the International Rules.

RULE #15

Crossing Situation

When two power-driven vessels are crossing so as to involve risk of collision, the vessel which has the other on her starboard side shall keep out of the way and shall, if the circumstances of the case admit, avoid crossing ahead of the other vessel.

RULE #16

Action By Give-Way Vessel

Every vessel which is directed to keep out of the way of another vessel shall, so far as possible, take early and substantial action to keep well clear.

RULE #17

Action By Stand-On Vessel

(a)(i) Where one of two vessels is to keep out of the way the other shall keep her course and speed.

(ii) The latter vessel may however take action to avoid collision by her maneuver alone, as soon as it becomes apparent to her that the vessel required to keep out of the way is not taking appropriate action in compliance with these Rules.

(b) When, from any cause, the vessel required to keep her course and speed finds herself so close that collision cannot be avoided by the action of the give-way vessel alone, she shall take such action as will best aid to avoid collision.

(c) A power-driven vessel which takes action in a crossing situation in accordance with subparagraph **(a)(ii)** of this Rule to avoid collision with another power-driven vessel shall, if the circumstances of the case admit, not alter course to port for a vessel on her own port side.

(d) This Rule does not relieve the give-way vessel of her obligation to keep out of the way.

INLAND RULE #15 - COMMENTS

15a) Vessels off the starboard side of another vessel are considered to have the right-of-way over another vessel.

15b) On the Great Lakes, Western Rivers and other Inland waterways, vessels travelling up and down a river have the right-of-way over any vessel attempting to cross said waterway. Nothing new here. That also applies to traffic fairways and traffic channels. Localized exceptions? Maybe. See Rule 10.

INLAND RULE #16 - COMMENTS

This Inland Rule is identical to the International Rule 16 and rather obvious.

INLAND RULE #17 - COMMENTS

International and Inland Rule 17 are identical. Please see Comments under International Rule 17.

When more than two vessels are meeting, it is termed "an exceptional circumstance" and none of the intersecting vessels has the right-of-way. The obvious alternative is to work it over carefully and avoid collision. Notice that the Rules regarding vessels on the approach are often prefaced by "when **two** vessels are approaching so as to..."

RULE #18

Responsibilities Between Vessels

Except where **Rules 9, 10, and 13** otherwise require:

(a) A power-driven vessel underway shall keep out of the way of:

(i) a vessel not under command;
(ii) a vessel restricted in her ability to maneuver;
(iii) a vessel engaged in fishing;
(iv) a sailing vessel.

(b) A sailing vessel underway shall keep out of the way of:

(i) a vessel not under command;
(ii) a vessel restricted in her ability to maneuver;
(iii) a vessel engaged in fishing.

(c) A vessel engaged in fishing when underway shall, so far as possible, keep out of the way of:

(i) a vessel not under command;
(ii) a vessel restricted in her ability to maneuver.

(d) A seaplane on the water shall, in general, keep well clear of all vessels and avoid impeding their navigation. In circumstances, however, where risk of collision exists, she shall comply with the Rules of this Part.

INLAND RULE #18 - COMMENTS

International and Inland Rule 18 are almost identical. Please see additional comments under Comments - International Rule 18.

The main exception between International and Inland is that the Inland Rules do not recognize "vessels constrained by their draft." That is, vessels which must navigate in narrow and/or shallow channels thereby having a special right-of-way.

See also page 102 for a graphic representation of the Pecking Order.

SECTION III-CONDUCT OF VESSELS IN RESTRICTED VISIBILITY

RULE #19

(a) This Rule applies to vessels not in sight of one another when navigating in or near an area of restricted visibility.

(b) Every vessel shall proceed at a safe speed adapted to the prevailing circumstances and conditions of restricted visibility. A power-driven vessel shall have her engines ready for immediate maneuver.

(c) Every vessel shall have due regard to the prevailing circumstances and conditions of restricted visibility when complying with Rules 4 through 10.

(d) A vessel which detects by radar the presence of another vessel shall determine if a close-quarters situation is developing or risk of collision exists. If so, she shall take avoiding action in ample time, provided that when such action consists of an alteration of course, so far as possible the following shall be avoided.

(i) an alteration of course to port for a vessel forward of the beam, other than for a vessel being overtaken;
(ii) an alteration of course towards a vessel abeam or abaft the beam.

(e) Except where it has been determined that a risk of collision does not exist, every vessel which hears apparently forward of her beam the fog signal of another vessel, or which cannot avoid a close-quarters situation with another vessel forward of her beam, shall reduce her speed to the minimum at which she can be kept on her course. She shall if necessary take all her way off and in any event navigate with extreme caution until danger of collision is over.

INLAND RULE #19 - COMMENTS

International and Inland Rule 19 are almost identical. The exceptions are some minor rewording. Please see Comments under International Rule 19.

PART C-LIGHTS AND SHAPES

RULE #20

Application

(a) Rules in this Part shall be complied with in all weathers.

(b) The Rules concerning lights shall be complied with from sunset to sunrise, and during such times no other lights shall be exhibited, except such lights as cannot be mistaken for the lights specified in these Rules or do not impair their visibility or distinctive character, or interfere with the keeping of a proper look-out.

(c) The lights prescribed by these Rules shall, if carried, also be exhibited from sunrise to sunset in restricted visibility and may be exhibited in all other circumstances when it is deemed necessary.

(d) The Rules concerning shapes shall be complied with by day.

(e) The lights and shapes specified in these Rules shall comply with the provisions of Annex I to the Rules.

INLAND RULE #20 - COMMENTS

International and Inland Rule 20 are almost identical. The exception is a one word difference and insignificant for test purposes. Please see Comments under the International Rules.

RULE #21

Definitions

(a) "Masthead light" means a white light placed over the fore and aft centerline of the vessel showing an unbroken light over an arc of the horizon of 225 degrees and so fixed as to show the light from right ahead to 22.5 degrees abaft the beam on either side of the vessel, except that on a vessel of less than 12 meters in length the masthead light shall be placed as nearly as practicable to the fore and aft centerline of the vessel.

(b) "Sidelights" means a green light on the starboard side and a red light on the port side each showing an unbroken light over an arc of the horizon of 112.5 degrees and so fixed as to show the light from right ahead to 22.5 degrees abaft the beam on its respective side. In a vessel of less than 20 meters in length the sidelights may be combined in one lantern carried on the fore and aft centerline of the vessel, except that on a vessel of less than 12 meters in length the sidelights when combined in one lantern shall be placed as nearly as practicable to the fore and aft centerline of the vessel.

(c) "Sternlight" means a white light placed as nearly as practicable at the stern showing an unbroken light over an arc of the horizon of 135 degrees and so fixed as to show the light 67.5 degrees from right aft on each side of the vessel.

(d) "Towing light" means a yellow light having the same characteristics as the "sternlight" defined in **paragraph (c)** of this Rule.

(Cont'd)

INLAND RULE #21 - COMMENTS

21a) International and Inland Rule 21 are almost identical. One of the differences with the masthead lights is that small power boats -less than 12 meters- do not necessarily have to have their masthead light located amidship.

NOTE: Sailboats (under sail) do not display a masthead light. However, once they light off that engine, Inland or International, they're technically powercraft and must show a masthead light.

21b) Combined sidelights are those combined with one bulb but with two Fresnel lenses. Anything less than 20 meters in length can do this Inland. Vessels less than 12 meters do not have to carry it exactly amidship. See pages 90-91.

21c-f, are identical to the International Rule 21. See Comments under International Rule 21.

21g) a "special flashing light" is used **only on the forward end** of barges being pushed ahead and then **only on Inland waters.** The arc is okay from 180 degrees to 225 degrees so the light can be mounted on the front of the barge below the main deck, or on the deck itself. Now see Rule 21f above and note the difference in timing of the flashes. 120 flashes vs. 50 to 70 flashes.

See also pages 100-101 for graphic breakdown of arcs and required visibilities. You need to know these pages for all Rules tests regardless of level of license sought.

RULE #21 (Cont'd)

(e) "All-round light" means a light showing an unbroken light over an arc of the horizon of 360 degrees.

(f) "Flashing light" means a light flashing at regular intervals at a frequency of 120 flashes or more per minute.

(g) "Special flashing light" means a yellow light flashing at regular intervals at a frequency of 50 to 70 flashes per minute, placed as far forward and as nearly as practicable on the fore and aft centerline of the tow and showing an unbroken light over an arc of the horizon of not less than 180 degrees nor more than 225 degrees and so fixed as to show the light from right ahead to abeam and no more than 22.5 degrees abaft the beam on either side of the vessel.

Rule 25(d)(ii) A vessel under oars may exhibit the lights prescribed in this Rule for sailing vessels, but if she does not, she shall have ready at hand an electric torch or lighted lantern showing a white light which shall be exhibited in sufficient time to prevent collision.

RULE #22

Visibility of Lights

The lights prescribed in these Rules shall have an intensity as specified in Annex I to these Rules, so as to be visible at the following minimum ranges:

(a) In vessels of 50 meters or more in length:
-a masthead light, 6 miles;
-a sidelight, 3 miles;
-a sternlight, 3 miles;
-a towing light, 3 miles;
-a white, red, green or yellow all-round light, 3 miles; and a special flashing light, 2 miles.

(b) In vessels of 12 meters or more in length but less than 50 meters in length:
-a masthead light, 5 miles; except that where the length of the vessel is less than 20 meters, 3 miles.
-a sidelight, 2 miles;
-a sternlight, 2 miles;
-a towing light, 2 miles;
-a white, red, green or yellow all-round light, 2 miles; and a special flashing light, 2 miles.
(c) In a vessel of less than 12 meters in length:
-a masthead light, 2 miles;
-a sidelight, 1 mile;
-a sternlight, 2 miles;
-a towing light, 2 miles;
-a white, red, green or yellow all-round light, 2 miles; and a special flashing light, 2 miles.

(d) In an inconspicuous, partly submerged vessels or object being towed:
-a white all-round light, 3 miles.

INLAND RULE #22 - COMMENTS

There is little difference between the definitions of lights as indicated in International Rule 22 and those of Inland Rule 22. The significant difference is the "special flashing light" on the bow of any barge being pushed ahead in Inland waters. The visibility required on this yellow light is 2 miles.

See also pages 100-101 for a graphic representation of the required visibility of lights.

RULE #23

Power-Driven Vessels Underway

(a) A power-driven vessel underway shall exhibit:

(i) a masthead light forward; except that a vessel of less than 20 meters in length need not exhibit this light forward of amidships but shall exhibit it as far forward as is practicable;

(ii) a second masthead light abaft of and higher than the forward one; except that a vessel of less than 50 meters in length shall not be obliged to exhibit such a light may do so;

(iii) sidelights; and

(iv) a sternlight.

(b) An air-cushion vessel when operating in the nondisplacement mode shall, in addition to the lights prescribed in **paragraph (a)** of this Rule, exhibit an all-round flashing yellow light where it can best be seen.

(c) A power-driven vessel of less than 12 meters in length may, in lieu of the lights prescribed in **paragraph (a)** of this Rule, exhibit an all-round white light and sidelights.

(d) A power-driven vessel when operating on the Great Lakes may carry an all-round white light in lieu of the second masthead light and sternlight prescribed in **paragraph (a)** of this Rule. The light shall be carried in the position of the second masthead light and be visible at the same minimum range.

INLAND RULE #23 - COMMENTS

There is a great deal of similarity between International and Inland Rule 23, but watch out. Read very carefully the Comments under International Rule 23 then note the comparison.

The runabout less than 7 meters making less than 7 knots does not appear in the Inland Rule 23.

Masthead lights and lights on air-cushion vessels are the same.

23c) Now we see the real differences concerning vessels which can use combined sidelights. Sailboats less than 20 meters can use combined sidelights and power craft less than 12 meters can use combined sidelights.

23d) The second masthead light (225°) is not required on the Great Lakes!! Instead, a lower all-round light can be used, but should be as high as the forward masthead light. Low bridges?

See also pages 90-91 and 100-101 for graphic representations of these arcs and visibilities.

▶⚓◀

RULE #24

Towing and Pushing

(a) A power-driven vessel when towing astern shall exhibit:
(i) instead of the light prescribed either in Rule **23(a)(i)** or **23(a)(ii)**, two masthead lights in a vertical line. When the length of the tow, measuring from the stern of the towing vessel to the after end of the tow exceeds 200 meters, three such lights in a vertical line;
(ii) sidelights;
(iii) a sternlight;
(iv) a towing light in a vertical line above the sternlight;
(v) when the length of the tow exceeds 200 meters, a diamond shape where it can best be seen.

(b) When a pushing vessel and a vessel being pushed ahead are rigidly connected in a composite unit they shall be regarded as a power-driven vessel and exhibit the lights prescribed in **Rule 23**.

(c) A power-driven vessel when pushing ahead or towing alongside, except as required by paragraphs **(b)** and **(i)** of this Rule shall exhibit:
(i) instead of the light prescribed either in **Rule 23(a)(i)** or **23(a)(ii)**, two masthead lights in a vertical line;
(ii) sidelights; and
(iii) two towing lights in a vertical line.

(d) A power-driven vessel to which **paragraphs (a)** or **(c)** of this Rule apply shall also comply with **Rule 23(a)(i)** and **23(a)(ii)**.

(e) A vessel or object other than those referred to in **paragraph (g)** of this Rule being towed shall exhibit:
(i) sidelights;
(ii) a sternlight; and
(iii) when the length of the tow exceeds 200 meters, a diamond shape where it can best be seen.

(Cont'd)

INLAND RULE #24 - COMMENTS

24a-f,i,j) Inland tugs tow astern under the same lighting arrangements as International. For a complete representation of tugs Inland and International see pages 90-99. Small boats towing someone in distress and don't ordinarily engage in towing, need not show the towing lights of the professionals, but should make their tow noticeable at night to anyone coming close.

Inland-when towing alongside or pushing ahead, things deviate from the International counterpart. When an Inland tug is **pushing ahead** or **towing alongside**, she must display **two** towing lights. (All "towing" lights are displayed astern). No white stern light is required. Pages 98-99.

The barge, only when pushed ahead, displays a "special flashing light" on the bow. The special flashing light is not used elsewhere in the Rules, either International or Inland. For a description of the special flashing light, see Inland Comments-Rule 21.

24g) Towing submerged or partially submerged articles Inland is almost the same as International. Basically, the difference is that the towing vessel may direct a searchlight at the tow to alert the passersby of the danger. Also, Inland Rules do not require a diamond dayshape at the front of the towed object, no matter what the length. One is required only at or near the after part of the last vessel in tow. International insists diamond dayshapes be visible fore **and** aft if towed over 200 meters astern.

RULE #24 (Cont'd)

(f) Provided that any number of vessels being towed alongside or pushed in a group shall be lighted as one vessel,

(i) a vessel being pushed ahead, not being part of a composite unit, shall exhibit at the forward end sidelights and a special flashing light; and

(ii) a vessel being towed alongside shall exhibit a sternlight and at the forward end sidelights.

(g) An inconspicuous, partly submerged vessel or object being towed, shall exhibit:

(i) if it is less than 25 meters in breadth, one all-round white light at or near each end.

(ii) if it is 25 meters or more in breadth, four all-round white lights to mark its length and breadth;

(iii) if it exceeds 100 meters in length, additional all-round white lights between the lights prescribed in **subparagraphs (i)** and **(ii)** so that the distance between the lights shall not exceed 100 meters: Provided, that any vessels or objects being towed alongside each other shall be lighted as one vessel or object;

(iv) a diamond shape at or near the aftermost extremity of the last vessel or object being towed; and

(v) the towing vessel may direct a searchlight in the direction of the tow to indicate its presence to an approaching vessel.

(h) Where from any sufficient cause it is impracticable for a vessel or object being towed to exhibit the lights or shapes prescribed in paragraph **(e)** or **(g)** of this Rule, all possible measures shall be taken to light the vessel or object towed or at least to indicate the presence of the unlighted vessel or object.

(Cont'd)

INLAND RULE #24 - COMMENTS

Rule #24(g) An inconspicuous, partly submerged vessel or object being towed, shall exhibit...

RULE #24 (Cont'd)

(i) Notwithstanding paragraph **(c)**, on the Western Rivers and on waters specified by the Secretary, a power-driven vessel when pushing ahead or towing alongside, except as paragraph **(b)** applies, shall exhibit:

(i) sidelights; and

(ii) two towing lights in a vertical line.

(j) Where from any sufficient cause it is impracticable for a vessel not normally engaged in towing operations to display the lights prescribed in paragraph (a),(c) or (i) of this Rule, such vessel shall not be required to exhibit those lights when engaged in towing another vessel in distress or otherwise in need of assistance. All possible measures shall be taken to indicate the nature of the relationship between the towing vessel and the vessel being assisted. The searchlight authorized by **Rule 36**, may be used to illuminate the tow.

INLAND RULE #24 - COMMENTS

Rule #15(b) Notwithstanding paragraph (a), on the Great Lakes, Western Rivers, or water specified by the Secretary, a vessel crossing a river shall keep out of the way of a power-driven vessel ascending or descending the river.

RULE #25

Sailing Vessels Underway and Vessels Under Oars

(a) A sailing vessel underway shall exhibit:
(i) sidelights;
(ii) a sternlight.

(b) In a sailing vessel of less than 20 meters in length the lights prescribed in paragraph **(a)** of this Rule may be combined in one lantern carried at or near the top of the mast where it can best be seen.

(c) A sailing vessel underway may, in addition to the lights prescribed in paragraph **(a)** of this Rule, exhibit at or near the top of the mast, where they can best be seen, two all-round lights in a vertical line, the upper being red and the lower green, but these lights shall not be exhibited in conjunction with the combined lantern permitted by paragraph **(b)** of this Rule.

(d)(i)
A sailing vessel of less than 7 meters in length shall, if practicable, exhibit the lights prescribed in paragraph **(a)** or **(b)** of this Rule, but if she does not, she shall have ready at hand an electric torch or lighted lantern showing a white light which shall be exhibited in sufficient time to prevent collision.
(ii) A vessel under oars may exhibit the lights prescribed in this Rule for sailing vessels, but if she does not, she shall have ready at hand an electric torch or lighted lantern showing a white light which shall be exhibited in sufficient time to prevent collision.

(e) A vessel proceeding under sail when also being propelled by machinery shall exhibit forward where it can best be seen a conical shape, apex downwards. A vessel of less than 12 meters in length is not required to exhibit this shape, but may do so.

INLAND RULE #25 - COMMENTS

International and Inland Rule 25 are identical. Please refer to Comments under International Rule 25.

RULE #26

Fishing Vessels

(a) A vessel engaged in fishing, whether underway or at anchor, shall exhibit only the lights and shapes prescribed in this Rule.

(b) A vessel when engaged in trawling, by which is meant the dragging through the water of a dredge net or other apparatus used as a fishing appliance, shall exhibit:

(i) two all-round lights in a vertical line, the upper being green and the lower white, or a shape consisting of two cones with their apexes together in a vertical line one above the other; a vessel less than 20 meters in length may instead of this shape exhibit a basket;

(ii) a masthead light abaft of and higher than the all-round green light; a vessel of less than 50 meters in length shall not be obliged to exhibit such a light but may do so;

(iii) when making way through the water, in addition to the lights prescribed in this paragraph, sidelights and a sternlight.

(c) A vessel engaged in fishing, other than trawling, shall exhibit:

(i) two all-round lights in a vertical line, the upper being red and the lower white, or a shape consisting of two cones with apexes together in a vertical line one above the other; a vessel of less than 20 meters in length may instead of this shape exhibit a basket;

(ii) when there is outlying gear extending more than 150 meters horizontally from the vessel, an all-round white light or a cone apex upwards in the direction of the gear;

(iii) when making way through the water, in addition to the lights prescribed in this paragraph, sidelights and a sternlight.

(d) A vessel engaged in fishing in close proximity to other vessels engaged in fishing may exhibit the additional signals described in Annex II to these Rules.

(e) A vessel when not engaged in fishing shall not exhibit the lights or shapes prescribed in this Rule, but only those prescribed for a vessel of her length.

INLAND RULE #26 - COMMENTS

International and Inland Rule 26 are identical, but most important for aspiring candidates. Please see Comments under International Rule 26.

RULE #27

Vessels Not Under Command or
Restricted In Their Ability to Maneuver

(a) A vessel not under command shall exhibit:

(i) two all-round red lights in a vertical line where they can best be seen;

(ii) two balls or similar shapes in a vertical line where they can best be seen;

(iii) when making way through the water, in addition to the lights prescribed in this paragraph, sidelights and a sternlight.

(b) A vessel restricted in her ability to maneuver, except a vessel engaged in minesweeping operations, shall exhibit:

(i) three all-round lights in a vertical line where they can best be seen. The highest and lowest of these lights shall be red and the middle light shall be white;

(ii) three shapes in a vertical line where they can best be seen. The highest and lowest of these shapes shall be balls and the middle one a diamond.

(iii) when making way through the water, a masthead light or lights, sidelights and a sternlight, in addition to the lights prescribed in **subparagraph (b)(i)**;and

(iv) when at anchor, in addition to the lights or shapes prescribed in **subparagraphs (b)(i)** and **(ii)**, the light, lights or shapes prescribed in **Rule 30.**

(c) A vessel engaged in a towing operation such as severely restricts the towing vessel and her tow in their ability to deviate from their course shall, in addition to the lights or shapes prescribed in **subparagraphs (b)(i)** and **(ii)** of this Rule, exhibit the lights or shape pesecribed in **Rule 24.**

(Cont'd)

INLAND RULE #27 - COMMENTS

International and Inland Rule 27 have some distinct similarities. Please see Comments found on pages 67 and 69. A further study of pages 90-99 will also show some subtle differences frequently exploited on CG exams.

RULE #27 (Con't)

(d) A vessel engaged in dredging or underwater operations when restricted in her ability to maneuver, shall exhibit the lights and shapes prescribed in **subparagraphs (b)(i), (ii)** and **(iii)** of the Rule and shall in addition, when an obstruction exists, exhibit:

(i) two all-round red lights or two balls in a vertical line to indicate the side on which the obstruction exists;

(ii) two all-round green lights or two diamonds in a vertical line to indicate the side on which another vessel may pass; and

(iii) when at anchor, the lights or shape prescribed by this paragraph instead of the lights or shape prescribed in **Rule 30**, for anchored vessels.

(e) Whenever the size of a vessel engaged in diving operations makes it impracticable to exhibit all lights and shapes prescribed in **paragraph (d)** of this Rule, the following instead shall be exhibited:

(i) Three all-round lights in a vertical line where they can best be seen. The highest and lowest of these lights shall be red and the middle light shall be white;

(ii) a rigid replica of the International Code flag "A" not less than 1 meter in height. Measures shall be taken to ensure its' all-round visibility.

(f) A vessel engaged in minesweeping operations shall in addition to the lights prescribed for a power-driven vessel in **Rule 23** or to the lights or shape prescribed for a vessel at anchore in **Rule 30** as appropriate, exhibit three all-round green lights or three balls. One of these lights or shapes shall be exhibited near the foremast head and one at each end of the fore yard. These lights or shapes indicate that it is dangerous for another vessel to approach within 1000 meters or 500 meters on either side of the minesweeper.

(Cont'd)

INLAND RULE #27 - COMMENTS

Rule #27(d) A vessel engaged in dredging or underwater operations when restricted in her ability to maneuver, shall exhibit the lights and shapes prescribed in subparagraphs (b)(i), (ii) and (iii) of the Rule and shall in addition when an obstruction exists, exhibit...

RULE #27 (Cont'd)

(g) A vessel of less than 12 meters in length, except those engaged in diving operations, shall not be required to exhibit the lights and shapes prescribed in this Rule.

(h) The signals prescribed in this Rule are not signals of vessels in distress and requiring assistance. Such signals are contained in **Annex IV** to these Rules.

RULE 28

There is no Rule 28 in Inland waters.

RULE 29

Pilot Vessels

29(a) A vessel engaged on pilotage duty shall exhibit:

(i) at or near the masthead, two all-round lights in a vertical line, the upper being white and the lower red;

(ii) when underway, in addition, sidelights and a sternlight; and

(iii) when at anchor, in addition to the lights prescribed in **subparagraph (i)**, the light, lights or shape prescribed in **Rule 30** for anchored vessels.

(b) A pilot vessel when not engaged on pilotage duty shall exhibit the lights or shapes prescribed for a similar vessel of her length.

INLAND RULE #28 - COMMENTS

While the Inland Rules do not "recognize" vessels constrained by draft in the open sense of the word, Rules are definitely in force preventing small craft from obstructing the passage of large cargo and working vessels in fairways, traffic patterns, etc. See Rules 9 and 10 for clearer definitions.

INLAND RULE #29 - COMMENTS

International and Inland Rule 29 are almost identical. Please see Comments under International Rule 29.

RULE #30

Anchored Vessels and Vessels Aground

(a) A vessel at anchor shall exhibit where it can best be seen:
(i) in the fore part, an all-round white light or one ball; and
(ii) at or near the stern and at a lower level than the light prescribed in **subparagraph (i)**, an all-round white light.

(b) A vessel of less than 50 meters in length may exhibit an all-round white light where it can best be seen instead of the lights prescribed in **paragraph (a)** of this Rule.

(c) A vessel at anchor may, and a vessel of 100 meters or more in length shall, also use the available working or equivalent lights to illuminate her decks.

(d) A vessel aground shall exhibit the lights prescribed in **paragraph (a)** or **(b)** of this Rule and in addition, if practicable, where they can best be seen:
(d)(i) two all-round red lights in a vertical line;
(d)(ii) three balls in a vertical line.

(e) A vessel of less than 7 meters in length, when at anchor, not in or near a narrow channel, fairway, anchorage, or where other vessels normally navigate, shall not be required to exhibit the lights or shape prescribed in **paragraphs (a)** and **(b)** of this Rule.

(f) A vessel of less than 12 meters in length, when aground, shall not be required to exhibit the lights or shapes prescribed in **subparagraphs (d)(i)** and **(ii)** of this Rule.

RULE 31

Seaplanes

Where it is impracticable for a seaplane to exhibit lights and shapes of the characteristics or in the positions prescribed in the Rules of this Part she shall exhibit lights and shapes as closely similar in characteristics and position as is possible.

INLAND RULE #30 - COMMENTS

International and Inland Rule 30 are almost identical. Please see Comments under International Rule 30 and note the difference indicated below.

Vessels less than 20 meters in length need show no anchor light in "special anchorages" designated by the Secretary of The Navy.

INLAND RULE #31 - COMMENTS

Obvious. No comments needed.

PART D - SOUND AND LIGHT SIGNALS

RULE #32

Definitions

(a) The word "whistle" means any sound signalling appliance capable of producing the prescribed blasts and which complies with the specifications in **Annex III** to these Rules.

(b) The term "short blast" means a blast of about one second's duration.

(c) The term "prolonged blast" means a blast of from 4 to 6 seconds' duration.

RULE #33

Equipment for Sound Signals

(a) A vessel of 12 meters or more in length shall be provided with a whistle and a bell and a vessel of 100 meters or more in length shall, in addition, be provided with a gong, the tone and sound of which cannot be confused with that of the bell. The whistle, bell and gong shall comply with the specifications in **Annex III** to these Regulations. The bell or gong or both may be replaced by other equipment having the same respective sound characteristics, provided that manual sounding of the prescribed signals shall always be possible.

(b) A vessel of less than 12 meters in length shall not be obliged to carry the sound signalling appliances prescribed in **paragraph (a)** of this Rule but if she does not, she shall be provided with some other means of making an efficient sound signal.

INLAND RULE #32-33 - COMMENTS

International and Inland Rules 32 and 33 are identical. Please see Comments under International Rules 32 and 33.

RULE #34

MANEUVERING AND WARNING SIGNALS

34(a) When power-driven vessels are in sight of one another and meeting or crossing at a distance within half a mile of each other, each vessel underway, when maneuvering as authorized or required by these Rules:
34(a)(i) shall indicate that maneuver by the following signals on her whistle: one short blast to mean "I intend to leave you on my port side"; two short blasts to mean "I intend to leave you on my starboard side"; and three short blasts to mean "I am operating astern propulsion".
34(a)(ii) Upon hearing the one or two blast signal of the other shall, if in agreement, sound the same whistle signal and take the steps necessary to effect a safe passing. If, however, from any cause, the vessel doubts the safety of the proposed maneuver, she shall sound the danger signal specified in paragraph (d) of this Rule and each vessel shall take appropriate precautionary action until a safe passing agreement is made.

34(b) A vessel may supplement the whistle signals prescribed in paragraph (a) of this Rule by light signals:
34(b)(i) These signals shall have the following significance: one flash to mean "I intend to leave you on my port side"; two flashes to mean "I intend to leave you on my starboard side"; three flashes to mean "I am operating astern propulsion";
34(b)(ii) the duration of each flash shall be about 1 second; and
34(b)(iii)) The light used for this signal shall, if fitted, be one all-round white or yellow light, visible at a minimum range of 2 miles, synchronized with the whistle, and shall comply with the provisions of Annex I to these Rules.

34(c) When in sight of one another:
34(c)(i) a power-driven vessel intending to overtake another power-driven vessel shall indicate her intention by the following signals on her whistle: one short blast to mean "I intend to overtake you on your starboard side"; two short blasts to mean "I intend to overtake you on your port side"; and

(Cont'd)

INLAND RULE #34 - COMMENTS

The comments relating to this rule are repeated here in the exact same sequence as they were in the International Comments. For exam module test purposes, there is no more important a rule than #34.

These signals are given in International waters when vessels are within sight of each other. In Inland waters the signals are given when vessels are within sight of each other **and when within a half-mile** of each other.

Herein lies one critical difference between International and Inland Rules. Note the whistle signals in the International context mean that when the signal is sounded **by** the **give-way** power-driven vessels the maneuver is already in progress. The maneuver **IS BEING CARRIED OUT.** Furthermore, no return signal from the **stand-on** craft is necessary. Another way of putting it is: if the vessel on International waters need not change course, no one or two blast signal is necessary.

This is not the case Inland. The whistle signals Inland mean you **intend** to execute a given maneuver. The stand-on vessel, upon hearing **either one or two blasts** from the give-way craft then **returns** the signal. **Then and only then, is the maneuver carried out.**

Again-in both Inland and International, the maneuvering signals are first sounded by the give-way craft.

An exception to this is in Inland waters when the downbound vessel **with a following current** has the right of way, is expected to sound the signals and choose the manner of crossing, overtaking, etc.

(Cont'd)

RULE #34 (Cont'd)

34(c)(ii) the power-driven vessel about to be overtaken shall, if in agreement, sound a similar sound signal. If in doubt she shall sound the danger signal prescribed in paragraph (d).

34(d) When vessels in sight of one another are approaching each other and from any cause either vessel fails to understand the intentions or actions of the other, or is in doubt whether sufficient action is being taken by the other to avoid collision, the vessel in doubt shall immediately indicate such doubt by giving at least five short and rapid blasts on the whistle. This signal may be supplemented by a light signal of at least five short and rapid flashes.

34(e) A vessel nearing a bend or an area of a channel or fairway where other vessels may be obscured by an intervening obstruction shall sound one prolonged blast. This signal shall be answered with a prolonged blast by any approaching vessel that may be within hearing around the bend or behind the intervening obstruction.

34(f) If whistles are fitted on a vessel at a distance apart of more than 100 meters, one whistle only shall be used for giving maneuvering and warning signals.

34(g) When a power-driven vessel is leaving a dock or berth, she shall sound one prolonged blast.

34(h) A vessel that reaches agreement with another vessel in a meeting, crossing, or overtaking situation by using the radio-telephone as prescribed by the Bridge-to-Bridge Radiotelephone Act (85 Stat.165; 33 U.S.C. 1207), is not obliged to sound the whistle signals prescribed by this Rule, but may do so. If agreement is not reached, then whistle signals shall be exchanged in a timely manner and shall prevail.

INLAND RULE #34 - COMMENTS

(Cont'd)

Be sure to have the overtaking signals down pat. There is a special signal for overtaking in a narrow channel in International waters which is not found in Inland waters. Also, on Inland waters, a vessel getting underway from a dock, pier or other mooring shall sound one prolonged blast.

The one prolonged blast is also sounded both Inland and International when vessels are approaching an obscured area caused by intervening obstructions. This signal is returned by anyone on the opposite approach.

Any maneuver, Inland or International, can be aborted by **any** vessel by sounding five or more short blasts on the whistle. The danger signal. The doubt signal.

These sound signals may be **supplemented** by light signals. But notice, the light used International is an all-round white light, but Inland is an all-round **yellow or white** light. An entire Rules of The Road quiz can be generated from the information relating to Rule 34.

Two last considerations. On Inland waters the radiotelephone can be substituted for initiating maneuvers to avoid collision, but not on International waters. All of the signals in Rule 34 pertain to **power-driven** vessels...not sailboats. Want it all summed up on one page? See p. 89.

RULE #35

Sound Signals in Restricted Visibility

(a) A power-driven vessel making way through the water shall sound at intervals of not more than 2 minutes one prolonged blast.

(b) A power-driven vessel underway but stopped and making no way through the water shall sound at intervals of not more than 2 minutes two prolonged blasts in succession with an interval of about 2 seconds between them.

(c) A vessel not under command; a vessel restricted in her ability to maneuver, whether underway or at anchor; a sailing vessel; a vessel engaged in fishing, whether underway or at anchor; and a vessel engaged in towing or pushing another vessel shall, instead of the signals prescribed in **paragraphs (a)** or **(b)** of this Rule, sound at intervals of not more than 2 minutes, three blasts in succession; namely, one prolonged followed by two short blasts.

(d) A vessel towed or if more than one vessel is towed the last vessel of the tow, if manned, shall at intervals of not more than 2 minutes sound four blasts in succession; namely one prolonged followed by three short blasts. When practicable, this signal shall be made immediately after the signal made by the towing vessel.

(e) When a pushing vessel and a vessel being pushed ahead are rigidly connected in a composite unit they shall be regarded as a power-driven vessel and shall give the signals prescribed in **paragraphs (a)** or **(b)** of this Rule.

(Cont'd)

INLAND RULE #35 - COMMENTS

A point often forgotten is that when moving into the realm of "restricted visibility" and especially dealing with sound signals, one must read again the titles to Section II commencing with Rule 11 **and** Part D commencing with Rule 32. The emphasis is that some signals are valid when vessels are within sight of each other, some in any condition visibility and now these sound signals in **restricted visibility.**

The point is this: The usual maneuvering signals are not sounded in restricted visibility. The danger (doubt) signal is **never** sounded in restricted visibility. Instead, a new set of signals and maneuvering conduct is available. The signals indicated are condensed on page 103 and when reading them notice the distinct difference in signals when underway as opposed to being anchored or aground. Notice particularly the time lapse required between signals when at anchor or aground vs. being underway.

RULE #35 (Cont'd)

(f) A vessel at anchor shall at intervals of not more than 1 minute ring the bell rapidly for about 5 seconds. In a vessel of 100 meters or more in length the bell shall be sounded in the forepart of the vessel and immediately after the ringing of the bell the gong shall be sounded rapidly for about 5 seconds in the after part of the vessel. A vessel at anchor may in addition sound three blasts in succession; namely, one short, one prolonged and one short blast, to give warning of her position and of the possibility of collision to an approaching vessel.

(g) A vessel aground shall give the bell signal and if required the gong signal prescribed in **paragraph (f)** of this Rule and shall, in addition, give three separate and distinct strokes on the bell immediately before and after the rapid ringing of the bell. A vessel aground may in addition sound an appropriate whistle signal.

(h) A vessel of less than 12 meters in length shall not be obliged to give the above-mentioned signals but, if she does not, shall make some other efficient sound signal at intervals of not more than 2 minutes.

(i) A pilot vessel when engaged on pilotage duty may in addition to the signals prescribed in **paragraph (a), (b)** or **(f)** of this Rule sound an identity signal consisting of four short blasts.

(j) The following vessels shall not be required to sound signals as prescribed in paragraph (f) of this Rule when anchored in a special anchorage area designated by the Secretary:

- **(i)** A vessel of less than 20 meters in length; and
- **(ii)** a barge, canal boat, scow, or other nondescript craft.

INLAND RULE #35 - COMMENTS

Rule #35(h) A vessel of less than 12 meters in length shall not be obliged to give the above-mentioned signals but, if she does not, shall make some other efficient sound signal at intervals of not more than 2 minutes.

RULE #36

Signals To Attract Attention

If necessary to attract the attention of another vessel, any vessel may make light or sound signals that cannot be mistaken for any signal authorized elsewhere in these Rules, or may direct the beam of her searchlight in the direction of the danger, in such a way as not to embarrass any vessel.

RULE #37

Distress Signals

When a vessel is in distress and requires assistance she shall use or exhibit the signals described in Annex IV to these Regulations.

The distress signals for inland waters are the same as those displayed on the previous page of this section for international waters with the following additional signal described:

A high intensity white light flashing at regular intervals from 50 to 70 times per minute.

INLAND RULE #36 - COMMENTS

This is like the International Rule. When trying to attract attention, don't shine your light into the pilot house of another vessel at night. Rough on night vision. It's called "embarrassing" the other craft. And note the Inland Rule, unlike the International Rule, makes no restriction against strobe lights and the likes.

INLAND RULE #37 - COMMENTS

The distress signals are indicated on page 104. They differ in one respect from International distress signals in that a white strobe light can be used flashing 50-70 flashes per minute.

PART E - EXEMPTIONS

RULE #38

Exemptions

Any vessel or class of vessels, the keel of which is laid or which is at a corresponding stage of construction before the date of enactment of this Act, provided that she complies with the requirements of-

(a) The act of June 7, 1897 (30 Stat. 96), as amended (33 U.S.C. 154-232) for vessels navigating the waters subject to that statute;

(b) Section 4233 of the Revised Statutes (33 U.S.C. 301-356) for vessels navigating the waters subject to that statute;

(c) The Act of February 8, 1895 (28 Stat. 645), as amended (33 U.S.C. 241-295) for vessels navigating the waters subject to that statute; or

(d) Sections 3,4, and 5 of the Act of April 25, 1940 (54 Stat. 163), as amended (46 U.S.C. 526 b,c, and d) for motorboats navigating the waters subject to that statute; shall be exempted from compliance with the technical Annexes to these Rules as follows:

(i) the installation of lights with ranges prescribed in Rule 22, until 4 years after the effective date of these Rules, except that vessels of less than 20 meters in length are permanently exempt;

(ii) the installation of lights with color specifications as prescribed in Annex I to these Rules, until 4 years after the effective date of these Rules, except that vessels of less than 20 meters in length are permanently exempt;

(Cont'd)

INLAND RULE #38 - COMMENTS

The exemptions detailed here speak for themselves, but boat owners in doubt are advised to contact the Coast Guard direct for a clearer picture. Always remember; don't buy advice from the Coast Guard, or for that matter from any other bureaucratic organization, over the phone. Get it in writing. That must particularly include any information you may call in for regarding a special circumstance for obtaining your license. Mo bettah you write them a short note and wait for the reply. But, make sure you have all of your questions ready and submit them at one time.

Of course, (ahem!) 99% of your questions can be answered in our text, *The Coast Guard License-From Six Pac to Master 100 Tons.* See the order form in the back of this volume.

Believe only half what you read and nothing you hear.

RULE #38 (Cont'd)

d(iii) the repositioning of lights as a result of conversion to metric units and rounding off measurement figures, are permanently exempt; and

(iv) the horizontal repositioning of masthead lights prescribed by Annex I to these Rules:

(1) on vessels of less than 150 meters in length, permanent exemption.

(2) on vessels of 150 meters or more in length, until 9 years after the effective date of these Rules.

(v) the restructuring or repositioning of all lights to meet the prescriptions of Annex I to these Rules, until 9 years after the effective date of these Rules;

(vi) power-driven vessels of 12 meters or more but less than 20 meters in length are permanently exempt from the provisions of Rule 23(a)(i) and 23(a)(iv) provided that, in place of these lights, the vessel exhibits a white light aft visible all round the horizon; and

(vii) the requirements for sound signal appliances prescribed in Annex III to these Rules, until 9 years after the effective date of these Rules.

ANNEX I

POSITIONING AND TECHNICAL DETAILS OF LIGHTS AND SHAPES

1) Definition

The term "height above the hull" means height above the uppermost continuous deck. This height shall be measured from the position vertically beneath the location of the light.

2) Vertical positioning and spacing of lights.

(a) On a power-driven vessel of 20 meters or more in length the masthead lights shall be placed as follows:

(i) the forward masthead light, or if only one masthead light is carried, then that light, at a height above the hull of not less than 6 meters, and, if the breadth of the vessel exceeds 6 meters, then at a height above the hull not less than such breadth, so however that the light need not be placed at a greater height above the hull than 12 meters;

(ii) *on a vessel of less than 20 meters in length such lights shall be spaced not less than 1 meter apart and the lowest of these lights shall, except where a towing light is required, be placed at a height of not less than 2 meters above the gunwale.*

(b) The vertical separation of masthead lights of power-driven vessels shall be such that in all normal conditions of trim the after light will be seen over and separate from the forward light at a distance of 1000 meters from the stem when viewed from sea level.

(c) The masthead light of a power-driven vessel of 12 meters but less than 20 meters in length shall be placed at a height above the gunwale of not less than 2.5 meters.

(d) A power-driven vessel of less than 12 meters in length may carry the uppermost light at a height of less than 2.5 meters above the gunwale. When however a masthead light is carried in addition to the sidelights and a sternlight *or the all-round light prescribed in rule 23(c)(i) is carried in addition to the sidelights*, then such masthead light *or all-round* light shall be carried at least 1 meter higher than the sidelights.

(e) One of the two or three masthead lights prescribed for a power-driven vessel when engaged in towing or pushing another vessel shall be placed in the same position as either the forward masthead light or the after masthead light; provided that, if carried on the aftermast, the lowest after masthead light shall be at least 4.5 meters vertically higher than the forward masthead light.

(f)(i) The masthead light or lights prescribed in Rule 23(a) shall be so placed as to be above and clear of all other lights and obstructions except as described in subparagraph (ii).

(ii) When it is impracticable to carry the all-round lights prescribed by Rule 27(b)(i) or Rule 28 below the masthead lights, they may be carried above the after masthead light(s) or vertically in between the forward masthead light(s) and after masthead light(s), provided that in the latter case the requirement of Section 3(c) of this Annex shall be complied with.

(g) The sidelights of a power-driven vessel shall be placed at a height above the hull not greater than three quarters of that of the forward masthead light. They shall not be so low as to be interfered with by deck lights.

(h) The sidelights, if in a combined lantern and carried on a power-driven vessel of less than 20 meters in length, shall be placed not less than 1 meter below the masthead light.

(i) When the Rules prescribe two or three lights to be carried in a vertical line, they shall be spaced as follows:

(i) on a vessel of 20 meters in length or more such lights shall be spaced not less than 2 meters apart, and the lowest of these lights shall, except where a towing light is required, be placed at a height of not less than 4 meters above the hull;

(ii) on a vessel of less than 20 meters in length such lights shall be spaced not less than 1 meter apart and the lowest of these lights shall, except where a towing light is required, be placed at a height of not less than 2 meters above the hull;

(iii) when three lights are carried they shall be equally spaced.

(j) the lower of the two all-round lights prescribed for a vessel when engaged in fishing shall be a height above the sidelights not less than twice the distance between the two vertical lights.

(k) The forward anchor light prescribed in Rule 30(a)(i), when two are carried, shall not be less than 4.5 meters above the after one. On a vessel of 50 meters or more in length this forward anchor light shall be placed at a height of not less than 6 meters above the hull.

3) Horizontal positioning and spacing of lights.

(a) When two masthead lights are prescribed for a power-driven vessel, the horizontal distance between them shall not be less than one half of the length of the vessel but need not be more than 100 meters. The forward light shall be placed not more than one quarter of the length of the vessel from the stem.

(b) On a power-driven vessel of 20 meters or more in length the sidelights shall not be placed in front of the forward masthead lights. They shall be placed at or near the side of the vessel.

(c) When the lights prescribed in Rule 27(b)(i) or Rule 28 are placed vertically between the forward masthead light(s) and the after masthead light(s) these all-round lights shall be placed at a horizontal distance of not less than 2 meters from the fore and aft centerline of the vessel in the athwartship direction.

4) Detail of location of direction-indicating lights for fishing vessels, dredgers and vessels engaged in underwater operations.

(a) The light indicating the direction of the outlying gear from a vessel engaged in fishing as prescribed in Rule 26(c)(ii) shall be placed at a horizontal distance of not less than 2 meters and not more than 6 meters away from the two all-round red and white lights. This light shall be placed not higher than the all-round white light prescribed in Rule 26(c)(i) and not lower than the sidelights.

(b) The lights and shapes on a vessel engaged in dredging or underwater operations to indicate the obstructed side and/or the side on which it is safe to pass, as prescribed in Rule 27(d)(i) and (ii), shall be placed at the maximum practical horizontal distance, but in no case less than 2 meters, from the lights or shapes prescribed in Rule 27(b)(i) and (ii). In no case shall the upper of these lights or shapes be at a greater height than the lower of the three lights or shapes prescribed in Rule 27(b)(i) and (ii).

5) Screens for sidelights.

The sidelights of vessels of 20 meters or more in length shall be fitted with inboard screens painted matt black, and meeting the requirements of Section 9 of this Annex. On vessels of less than 20 meters in length the sidelights, if necessary to meet the requirements of Section 9 of this Annex, shall be fitted with inboard matt black screens. With a combined lantern, using a single vertical filament and a very narrow division between the green and red sections, external screens need not be fitted.

6) Shapes

(a) Shapes shall be black and of the following sizes:

(i) a ball shall have a diameter of not less than 0.6 meter;

(ii) a cone shall have a base diameter of not less than 0.6 meter and a height equal to its diameter;

(iii) a cylinder shall have a diameter of at least 0.6 meter and a height of twice its diameter;

(iv) a diamond shape shall consist of two cones as defined in (ii) above having a common base.

(b) The vertical distance between shapes shall be at least 1.5 meter.

(c) In a vessel of less than 20 meters in length shapes of lesser dimensions but commensurate with the size of the vessel may be used and the distance apart may be correspondingly reduced.

7) Color specification of lights.

The chromaticity of all navigation lights shall conform to the following standards, which lie within the boundaries of the area of the diagram specified for each color by the International Commission on Illumination (CIE).

The boundaries of the area for each color are given by indicating the corner coordinates, which are as follows:

(i) White:

x	0.525	0.525	0.452	0.310	0.310	0.443
y	0.382	0.440	0.440	0.348	0.283	0.382

(ii) Green:

x	0.028	0.009	0.300	0.203
y	0.385	0.723	0.511	0.356

(iii) Red:

x	0.680	0.660	0.735	0.721
y	0.320	0.320	0.265	0.259

(iv) Yellow:

x	0.612	0.618	0.575	0.575
y	0.382	0.382	0.425	0.406

8) Intensity of lights.

(a) The minimum luminous intensity of lights shall be calculated by using the formula:
$I=3.43 \times 10^6 \times T \times D^2 \times K^{-D}$
where I is luminous intensity in candelas under service conditions,
T is threshold factor 2×10^{-7} lux,
D is range of visibility (luminous range) of the light in nautical miles,
K is atmospheric transmissivity. For prescribed lights the value of K shall be 0.8, corresponding to a meteorological visibility of approximately 13 nautical miles.

(b) A selection of figures derived from the formula is given in the following table:

Range of visibility (luminous range) of light in nautical miles D	Luminous intensity of light in candelas for K=0.8 I
1	0.9
2	4.3
3	12
4	27
5	52
6	94

Note: The maximum luminous intensity of navigation lights should be limited to avoid undue glare. This shall not be achieved by a variable control of the luminous intensity.

9) Horizontal sectors.

(a)(i) In the forward direction, sidelights as fitted on the vessel shall show the minimum required intensities. The intensities shall decrease to reach practical cut-off between 1 degree and 3 degrees outside the prescribed sectors.

(ii) For sternlights and masthead lights and at 22.5 degrees abaft the beam for sidelights, the minimum required intensities shall be maintained over the arc of the horizon up to 5 degrees within the limits of the sectors prescribed in Rule 21. From 5 degrees with the prescribed sectors the intensity may decrease by 50 percent up to the prescribed limits; it shall decrease steadily to reach practical cut-off at not more than 5 degrees outside the prescribed sectors.

(b) All-round lights shall be so located as not to be obscured by masts, topmasts or structures within angular sectors of more than 6 degrees, except anchor lights prescribed in Rule 30 which need not be placed at an impracticable height above the hull.

10) Vertical sectors.

(a) The vertical sectors of electric lights as fitted, with the exception of lights on sailing vessels *under sail* shall ensure that:

(i) at least the required minimum intensity is maintained at all angles from 5 degrees above to 5 degrees below the horizontal;

(ii) at least 60 percent of the required minimum intensity is maintained from 7.5 degrees above to 7.5 degrees below the horizontal.

(b) In the case of sailing vessels *under sail* the vertical sectors of electric lights as fitted shall ensure that:

(i) at least the required minimum intensity is maintained at all angles from 5 degrees above to 5 degrees below the horizontal;

(ii) at least 50 percent of the required minimum intensity is maintained from 25 degrees above to 25 degrees below the horizontal.

(c) In the case of lights other than electric these specifications shall be met as closely as possible.

11) Intensity of non-electric lights.

Non-electric lights shall so far as practicable comply with the minimum intensities, as specified in the Table given in Section 8 of this Annex.

12) Maneuvering light.

Notwithstanding the provisions of paragraph 2(f) of this Annex the maneuvering lights described in Rule 34(b) shall be placed in the same fore and aft vertical plane as the masthead light or lights and, where practicable, at a minimum height of 2 meters vertically above the forward masthead light, provided that it shall be carried not less than 2 meters vertically above or below the after masthead light. On a vessel where only one masthead light is carried the maneuvering light, if fitted, shall be carried where it can best be seen, not less than 2 meters vertically apart from the masthead light.

13) Approval.

The construction of lights and shapes and the installation of lights on board the vessel shall be to the satisfaction of the appropriate authority of the State whose flag the vessel is entitled to fly.

ANNEX II

ADDITIONAL SIGNALS FOR FISHING VESSELS FISHING IN CLOSE PROXIMITY

1) General

The lights mentioned herein shall, if exhibited in pursuance of Rule 26(d), be placed where they can best be seen. They shall be at least 0.9 meter apart but at a lower level than lights prescribed in Rule 26(b)(i) and (c)(i). The lights shall be visible all around the horizon at a distance of at least 1 mile but at a lesser distance from the lights prescribed by these Rules for fishing vessels.

2) Signals for trawlers

(a) Vessels when engaged in trawling, whether using demersal or pelagic gear, may exhibit:

(i) when shooting their nets: two white lights in a vertical line;

(ii) when hauling their nets: one white light over one red light in a vertical line;

(iii) when the net has come fast upon an obstruction: two red lights in a vertical line.

(b) Each vessel engaged in pair trawling may exhibit:

(i) by night, a searchlight directed forward and in the direction of the other vessel of the pair;

(ii) when shooting or hauling their nets or when their nets have come fast upon an obstruction, the lights prescribed in 2(a) above.

3) Signals for purse seiners

Vessels engaged in fishing with purse seine gear may exhibit two yellow lights in a vertical line. These lights shall flash alternately every second and with equal light and occultation duration. These lights may be exhibited only when the vessel is hampered by its fishing gear.

ANNEX III

TECHNICAL DETAILS OF SOUND SIGNAL APPLIANCES

1) Whistles

(a) Frequencies and range of audibility. The fundamental frequency of the signal shall lie within the range of 70-700 Hz.
The range of audibility of the signal from a whistle shall be determined by those frequencies, which may include the fundamental and/or one or more higher frequencies, which lie within the range 180-700Hz (1 percent) and which provide the sound pressure levels specified in paragraph 1(c) below.

(b) Limits of fundamental frequencies. To ensure a wide variety of whistle characteristics, the fundamental frequency of a whistle shall be between the following limits:
(i) 70-200 Hz, for a vessel 200 meters or more in length;
(ii) 130-350 Hz, for a vessel 75 meters but less than 200 meters in length;
(iii) 250-700 Hz, for a vessel less than 75 meters in length.

(c) Sound signal intensity and range of audibility. A whistle fitted in a vessel shall provide, in the direction of maximum intensity of the whistle and at a distance of 1 meter from it, a sound pressure level in at least one 1/3-octave band within the range of frequencies 180-700 Hz (1 percent) of not less than the appropriate figure given in the table below.

Length of vessel in meters	1/3 -octave band level at 1 meter in dB referred to $2x10^{-5}$ N/m^2	Audibility range in nautical miles
200 or more	143	2.0
75 but less than 200	138	1.5
20 but less than 75	130	1.0
Less than 20	120	0.5

The range of audibility in the table above is for information and is approximately the range at which a whistle may be heard on its forward axis with 90 percent probability in conditions of still air on board a vessel having average background noise level at the listening posts (taken to be 68 dB in the octave band centered on 250 Hz and 63 dB in the octave band centered on 500 Hz).
In practice the range at which a whistle may be heard is extremely variable and depends critically on weather conditions; the values given can be regarded as typical but under conditions of strong wind or high ambient noise level at the listening post the range may be much reduced.

(d) Directional properties. The sound pressure level of a directional whistle shall be not more than 4 dB below the prescribed sound pressure level on the axis at any direction in the horizontal plane within plus or minus 45 degrees of the axis. The sound pressure level at any other direction in the horizontal plane shall be not more that 10 dB below the prescribed sound pressure level on the axis, so that the range in any direction will be at least half the range on the forward axis. The sound pressure level shall be measured in that one-third octave band which determines the audibility range.

(e) Positioning of whistles. When a directional whistle is to be used as the only whistle on a vessel, it shall be installed with its maximum intensity directed straight ahead.

A whistle shall be placed as high as practicable on a vessel, in order to reduce interception of the emitted sound by obstructions and also to minimize hearing damage risk to personnel. The sound pressure level of the vessel's own signal at listening posts shall not exceed 110 dB(A) and so far as practicable should not exceed 100 dB(A).

(f) Fitting of more than one whistle. If whistles are fitted at a distance apart of more than 100 meters, it shall be so arranged that they are not sounded simultaneously.

(g) Combined whistle systems. If due to the presence of obstructions the sound field of a single whistle or of one of the whistles referred to in paragraph 1(f) above is likely to have a zone of greatly reduced signal level, it is recommended that a combined whistle system be fitted so as to overcome this reduction. For the purposes of the Rules a combined whistle system is to be regarded as a single whistle. The whistles of a combined system shall be located at a distance apart of not more than 100 meters and arranged to be sounded simultaneously. The frequency of any one whistle shall differ from those of the others by at least 10 Hz.

2) Bell or gong

(a) Intensity of signal. A bell or gong, or other device having similar sound characteristics shall produce a sound pressure level of not less than 110 dB at a distance of 1 meter from it.

(b) Construction. Bells and gongs shall be made of corrosion-resistant material and designed to give a clear tone. The diameter of the mouth of the bell shall be not less than 300 mm for vessels of 20 meters or more in length, and shall be not less than 200 mm for vessels of 12 meters or more but of less than 20 meters in length. Where practicable, a power-driven bell striker is recommended to ensure constant force but manual operation shall be possible. The mass of the striker shall be not less than 3 percent of the mass of the bell.

3) Approval. The construction of sound signal appliances, their performance and their installation on board the vessel shall be to the satisfaction of the appropriate authority of the State whose flag the vessel is entitled to fly.

ANNEX IV

DISTRESS SIGNALS

1. Need of assistance

The following signals, used or exhibited either together or separately, indicate distress and need of assistance:
a) a gun or other explosive signal fired at intervals of about a minute;
b) a continuous sounding with any fog-signalling apparatus;
c) rockets or shells, throwing red stars fired one at a time at short intervals;
d) a signal made by radiotelegraphy or by any other signalling method consisting of the group ··· — — — ··· (SOS) in the Morse Code;
e) a signal sent by radiotelephony consisting of the spoken word "Mayday";
f) the International Code Signal of distress indicated by N.C.;
g) a signal consisting of a square flag having above or below it a ball or anything resembling a ball;
h) flames on the vessel (as from a burning tar barrel, oil barrel, etc.);
i) a rocket parachute flare or a hand flare showing a red light;
j) a smoke signal giving off orange-colored smoke;
k) slowly and repeatedly raising and lowering arms outstretched to each side;
l) the radiotelegraph alarm signal;
m) the radiotelephone alarm signal;
n) signals transmitted by emergency position-indicating radio beacons.
o) approved signal transmitted by radio communications system.

2. The use or exhibition of any of the foregoing signals except for the purpose of indicating distress and need of assistance and the use of other signals which may be confused with any of the above signals is prohibited.

3. Attention is drawn to the relevant sections of the International Code of Signals, the Merchant Ship Search and Rescue Manual and the following signal:

(a) a piece of orange-colored canvas with either a black square and circle or other appropriate symbol (for identification from the air);

(b) a dye marker.

ANNEX I

POSITIONING AND TECHNICAL DETAILS OF LIGHTS AND SHAPES

§ 84.01 Definitions

(a) The term "height above the hull" means height above the uppermost continuous deck. This height shall be measured from the position vertically beneath the location of the light.
(b) The term "practical cut-off" means, for vessels 20 meters or more in length, 12.5 percent of the minimum luminous intensity (Table 84.15(b)) corresponding to the greatest range of visibility for which the requirements of Annex I are met.
(c) The term "Rule" or "Rules" means the Inland Navigation Rules contained in Sec. 2 of the Inland Navigational Rules Act of 1980 (Pub. L. 96-591, 94 Stat. 3415, 33 U.S.C. 2001, December 24, 1980) as amended.

§ 84.03 Vertical positioning and spacing of lights.

(a) On a power-driven vessel of 20 meters or more in length the masthead lights shall be placed as follows:
(1) The forward masthead light, or if only one masthead light is carried, then that light, at a height above the hull of not less than 5 meters, and, if the breadth of the vessel exceeds 5 meters, then at a height above the hull not less than such breadth, so however that the light need not be placed at a greater height above the hull than 8 meters;
(2) When two masthead lights are carried the after one shall be at least 2 meters vertically higher than the forward one.

(b) The vertical separation of masthead lights of power-driven vessels shall be such that in all normal conditions of trim the after light will be seen over and separate from the forward light at a distance of 1000 meters from the stem when viewed from water level.

(c) The masthead light, of a power-driven vessel of 12 meters but less than 20 meters in length shall be placed at a height above the gunwale of not less than 2.5 meters.

(d) The masthead light, or the all-round light described in Rule 23(c), of a power-driven vessel of less than 12 meters in length shall be carried at least one meter higher than the sidelights.

(e) One of the two or three masthead lights prescribed for a power-driven vessel when engaged in towing or pushing another vessel shall be placed in the same position as either the forward masthead light or the after masthead light, provided that the lowest after masthead light shall be at least 2 meters vertically higher than the highest forward masthead light.

(f)(1) The masthead light or lights prescribed in Rule 23(a) shall be so placed as to be above and clear of all other lights and obstructions except as described in paragraph (f)(2) of this section.

(2) When it is impracticable to carry the all-round lights prescribed in Rule 27(b)(i) below the masthead lights, they may be carried above the after masthead light(s) or vertically in between the forward masthead light(s) and after masthead light(s), provided that in the latter case the requirement of 84.05(d) shall be complied with.

(g) The sidelights of a power-driven vessel shall be placed at least one meter lower than the forward masthead light. They shall not be so low as to be interfered with by deck lights.

(h) (Reserved)

(i) When the Rules prescribe two or three lights to be carried in a vertical line, they shall be spaced as follows:

(1) on a vessel of 20 meters in length or more such lights shall be spaced not less than 1 meter apart, and the lowest of these lights shall, except where a towing light is required, be placed at a height of not less than 4 meters above the hull;

(2) on a vessel of less than 20 meters in length such lights shall be spaced not less than 1 meter apart and the lowest of these lights shall, except where a towing light is required, be placed at a height of not less than 2 meters above the hull;

(3) when three lights are carried they shall be equally spaced.

(j) the lower of the two all-round lights prescribed for a vessel when engaged in fishing shall be at a height above the sidelights not less than twice the distance between the two vertical lights.

(k) The forward anchor light prescribed in Rule 30(a)(i), when two are carried, shall not be less than 4.5 meters above the after one. On a vessel of 50 meters or more in length this forward anchor light shall be placed at a height of not less than 6 meters above the hull.

§ 84.05 Horizontal positioning and spacing of lights.

(a) Except as specified in paragraph (b) of this section, when two masthead lights are prescribed for a power-driven vessel, the horizontal distance between them shall not be less than one quarter of the length of the vessel but need not be more than 50 meters. The forward light shall be placed not more than one half of the length of the vessel from the stem.

(b) On a power-driven vessel of 50 meters, but less than 60 meters in length operated on the Western Rivers, the horizontal distance between masthead lights shall not be less than 10 meters.

(c) On a power-driven vessel of 20 meters or more in length the sidelights shall not be placed in front of the forward masthead lights. They shall be placed at or near the side of the vessel.

(d) When the lights prescribed in Rule 27(b)(i) are placed vertically between the forward masthead light(s) and the after masthead light(s) these all-round lights shall be placed at a horizontal distance of not less than 2 meters from the fore and aft centerline of the vessel in the athwartship direction.

§ 84.07 Details of location of direction-indicating lights for fishing vessels, dredgers and vessels engaged in underwater operations.

(a) The light indicating the direction of the outlying gear from a vessel engaged in fishing as prescribed in Rule 26(c)(ii) shall be placed at a horizontal distance of not less than 2 meters and not more than 6 meters away from the two all-round red and white lights. This light shall be placed not higher than the all-round white light prescribed in Rule 26(c)(i) and not lower than the sidelights.

(b) The lights and shapes on a vessel engaged in dredging or underwater operations to indicate the obstructed side and/or the side on which it is safe to pass, as prescribed in Rule 27(d)(i) and (ii), shall be placed at the maximum practical horizontal distance, but in no case less than 2 meters, from the lights or shapes prescribed in Rule 27(b)(i) and (ii). In no case shall the upper of these lights or shapes be at a greater height than the lower of the three lights or shapes prescribed in Rule 27(b)(i) and (ii).

§ 84.09 Screens

(a) The sidelights of vessels of 20 meters or more in length shall be fitted with matt black inboard screens and meet the requirements of 84.17. On vessels of less than 20 meters in length the sidelights, if necessary to meet the requirements of 84.17, shall be fitted with matt black inboard screens. With a combined lantern, using a single vertical filament and a very narrow division between the green and red sections, external screens need not be fitted.

(b) On power-driven vessels less than 12 meters in length constructed after July 31, 1983, the masthead light, or the all-round light described in Rule 23(c) shall be screened to prevent direct illumination of the vessel forward of the operator's position.

§ 84.11 Shapes

(a) Shapes shall be black and of the following sizes:

(1) a ball shall have a diameter of not less than 0.6 meter;

(2) a cone shall have a base diameter of not less than 0.6 meter and a height equal to its diameter;

(3) a diamond shape shall consist of two cones (as defined in paragraph (a)(2) of this section) having a common base.

(b) The vertical distance between shapes shall be at least 1.5 meter.

(c) In a vessel of less than 20 meters in length shapes of lesser dimensions but commensurate with the size of the vessel may be used and the distance apart may be correspondingly reduced.

§ 84.13 Color specification of lights.

(a) The chromaticity of all navigation lights shall conform to the following standards, which lie within the boundaries of the area of the diagram specified for each color by the International Commission on Illumination (CIE), in the "Colors of Light Signals", which is incorporated by reference. It is Publication CIE No. 2.2. (TC-1.6), 1975, and is available from the Illumination Engineering Society, 345 East 47th Street, New York , N.Y. 10017. It is also available for inspection at the Office of the Federal Register, Room 8401, 1100 L Street N.W., Washington, D.C. 20408. This incorporation by reference was approved by the Director of the Federal Register.

(b) The boundaries of the area for each color are given by indicating the corner coordinates, which are as follows:

(1) White:

x	0.525	0.525	0.452	0.310	0.310	0.443
y	0.382	0.440	0.440	0.348	0.283	0.382

(2) Green:

x	0.028	0.009	0.300	0.203
y	0.385	0.723	0.511	0.356

(3) Red:

x	0.680	0.660	0.735	0.721
y	0.320	0.320	0.265	0.259

(4) Yellow:

x	0.612	0.618	0.575	0.575
y	0.382	0.382	0.425	0.406

§ 84.15 Intensity of lights.

(a) The minimum luminous intensity of lights shall be calculated by using the formula:
$I=3.43 \times 10^{6} \times T \times D^{2} \times K^{-D}$
where I is luminous intensity in candelas under service conditions,
T is threshold factor 2×10^{-7} lux,
D is range of visibility (luminous range) of the light in nautical miles,
K is atmospheric transmissivity. For prescribed lights the value of K shall be 0.8, corresponding to a meteorological visibility of approximately 13 nautical miles.

(b) A selection of figures derived from the formula is given in table 84.15(b).

Table 84.15(b)

Range of visibility (luminous range) of light in nautical miles D	Luminous intensity of light in candelas for K=0.8 I
1	0.9
2	4.3
3	12
4	27
5	52
6	94

§ 84.17 Horizontal sectors.

(a)(1) In the forward direction, sidelights as fitted on the vessel shall show the minimum required intensities. The intensities shall decrease to reach practical cut-off between 1 and 3 degrees outside the prescribed sectors.

(2) For sternlights and masthead lights and at 22.5 degrees abaft the beam for sidelights, the minimum required intensities shall be maintained over the arc of the horizon up to 5 degrees within the limits of the sectors prescribed in Rule 21. From 5 degrees with the prescribed sectors the intensity may decrease by 50 percent up to the prescribed limits; it shall decrease steadily to reach practical cut-off at not more than 5 degrees outside the prescribed sectors.

(b) All-round lights shall be so located as not to be obscured by masts, topmasts or structures within angular sectors of more than 6 degrees, except anchor lights prescribed in Rule 30 which need not be placed at an impracticable height above the hull, and the all-round white light described in Rule 23(d), which may not be obscured at all.

(a) The vertical sectors of electric lights as fitted, with the exception of lights on sailing vessels and on unmanned barges, shall ensure that:

(1) at least the required minimum intensity is maintained at all angles from 5 degrees above to 5 degrees below the horizontal;

(2) at least 60 percent of the required minimum intensity is maintained from 7.5 degrees above to 7.5 degrees below the horizontal.

(b) In the case of sailing vessels the vertical sectors of electric lights as fitted shall ensure that:

(1) at least the required minimum intensity is maintained at all angles from 5 degrees above to 5 degrees below the horizontal;

(2) at least 50 percent of the required minimum intensity is maintained from 25 degrees above to 25 degrees below the horizontal.

(c) In the case of unmanned barges the minimum required intensity of electric lights as fitted shall be maintained on the horizontal.

(d) In the case of lights other than electric lights these specifications shall be met as closely as possible.

§ 84.21 Intensity of non-electric lights.

Non-electric lights shall so far as practicable comply with the minimum intensities, as specified in the Table given in § 84.15.

§ 84.23 Maneuvering light.

Notwithstanding the provisions of § 84.03(f), the maneuvering lights described in Rule 34(b) shall be placed approximately in the same fore and aft vertical plane as the masthead light or lights and, where practicable, at a minimum height of one-half meter vertically above the forward masthead light, provided that it shall be carried not less than one-half meter vertically above or below the after masthead light. On a vessel where only one masthead light is carried the maneuvering light, if fitted, shall be carried where it can best be seen, not less than one-half meter vertically apart from the masthead light.

§ **84.25 Approval.** (Reserved).

ANNEX II

ADDITIONAL SIGNALS FOR FISHING VESSELS FISHING IN CLOSE PROXIMITY

§ 85.1 General

The lights mentioned herein shall, if exhibited in pursuance of Rule 26(d), be placed where they can best be seen. They shall be at least 0.9 meter apart but at a lower level than lights prescribed in Rule 26(b)(i) and (c)(i) contained in the Inland Navigational Rules Act of 1980. The lights shall be visible all around the horizon at a distance of at least 1 mile but at a lesser distance from the lights prescribed by these Rules for fishing vessels.

§ 85.3 Signals for trawlers

(a) Vessels when engaged in trawling, whether using demersal or pelagic gear, may exhibit:

(1) When shooting their nets: two white lights in a vertical line;

(2) When hauling their nets: one white light over one red light in a vertical line;

(3) When the net has come fast upon an obstruction: two red lights in a vertical line.

(b) Each vessel engaged in pair trawling may exhibit:

(1) By night, a searchlight directed forward and in the direction of the other vessel of the pair;

(2) When shooting or hauling their nets or when their nets have come fast upon an obstruction, the lights prescribed in paragraph (a) above.

§ 85.5 Signals for purse seiners

Vessels engaged in fishing with purse seine gear may exhibit two yellow lights in a vertical line. These lights shall flash alternately every second and with equal light and occultation duration. These lights may be exhibited only when the vessel is hampered by its fishing gear.

ANNEX III

TECHNICAL DETAILS OF SOUND SIGNAL APPLIANCES

SUBPART A - Whistles

§ 86.01 Frequencies and range of audibility.

The fundamental frequency of the signal shall lie within the range 70-525 Hz. The range of audibility of the signal from a whistle shall be determined by those frequencies, which may include the fundamental and/or one or more higher frequencies, which lie within the frequency ranges and provide the sound pressure levels specified in 86.05.

§ 86.03 Limits of fundamental frequencies.

To ensure a wide variety of whistle characteristics, the fundamental frequency of a whistle shall be between the following limits:

(a) 70-200 Hz, for a vessel 200 meters or more in length;

(b) 130-350 Hz, for a vessel 75 meters but less than 200 meters in length;

(c) 250-525 Hz, for a vessel less than 75 meters in length.

§ 86.05 Sound signal intensity and range of audibility.

A whistle on a vessel shall provide, in the direction of the forward axis of the whistle and at a distance of 1 meter from it, a sound pressure level in at least one 1/3-octave band of not less than the appropriate figure given in Table 86.05 within the following frequency ranges (1 percent):

(a) 130-1200 Hz, for a vessel 75 meters or more in length;

(b) 250-1600 Hz, for a vessel 20 meters but less than 75 meters in length;

(c) 250-2100 Hz, for a vessel 12 meters but less than 20 meters in length.

Table 86.05

Length of vessel in meters	Fundamental frequency range (Hz)	For measured frequencies (Hz)	⅓-octave band level at 1 meter in dB referred to $2x10^{-5}$ N/m^2	Audibility range in nautical miles
200 or more	70-200	130-180*	145	2
		180-250*	143	
		250-120*	140	
75 but less than 200	130-250	130-180*	140	1.5
		180-250*	138	
		250-1200*	134	
20 but less than 75	250-525	250-450*	130	1.0
		450-800*	125	
		800-1600*	121	
12 but less than 20	250-525	250-450*	120	0.5
		450-800*	115	
		800-2100*	111	

Note: The range of audibility in the table above is for information and is approximately the range at which a whistle may usually be heard on its forward axis in conditions of still air on board a vessel having average background noise level at the listening posts (taken to be 68 dB in the octave band centered on 250 Hz and 63 dB in the octave band centered on 500 Hz).

In practice the range at which a whistle may be heard is extremely variable and depends critically on weather conditions; the values given can be regarded as typical but under conditions of strong wind or high ambient noise level at the listening post the range may be reduced.

§ **86.07 Directional properties.** The sound pressure level of a directional whistle shall be not more than 4 dB below the sound pressure level specified in 86.05 in any direction in the horizontal plane within plus or minus 45 degrees of the forward axis. The sound pressure level of the whistle at any other direction in the horizontal plane shall not be more than 10 dB less than the sound pressure level specified for the forward axis, so that the range of audibility in any direction will be at least half the range required on the forward axis. The sound pressure level shall be measured in that one-third octave band which determines the audibility range.

§ **86.09 Positioning of whistles.**

(a) When a directional whistle is to be used as the only whistle on the vessel and is permanently installed, it shall be installed with its forward axis directed forward.

(b) A whistle shall be placed as high as practicable on a vessel, in order to reduce interception of the emitted sound by obstructions and also to minimize hearing damage risk to personnel. The sound pressure level of the vessel's own signal at listening posts shall not exceed 110 dB(A) and so far as practicable should not exceed 100 dB(A).

§ **86.11 Fitting of more than one whistle.** If whistles are fitted at a distance apart of more than 100 meters, they shall not be sounded simultaneously.

§ **86.13 Combined whistle systems.**

(a) A combined whistle system is a number of whistles (sound emitting sources) operated together. For the purposes of the Rules a combined whistle system is to be regarded as a single whistle.

(b) The whistles of a combined system shall-

(1) Be located at a distance apart of not more than 100 meters,

(2) Be sounded simultaneously,

(3) Each have a fundamental frequency different from those of the others by at least 10 Hz, and

(4) Have a tonal characteristic appropriate for the length of vessel which shall be evidenced by at least two-thirds of the whistles in the combined system having fundamental frequencies falling within the limits prescribed in § 86.03, or if there are only two whistles in the combined system, by the higher fundamental frequency falling within the limits prescribed in § 86.03.

NOTE: If due to the presence of obstructions the sound field of a single whistle or of one of the whistles referred to in § 86.11 is likely to have a zone of greatly reduced signal level, a combined whistle system should be fitted so as to overcome this reduction.

§ 86.15 Towing vessel whistles.

A power-driven vessel normally engaged in pushing ahead or towing alongside may, at all times, use a whistle whose characteristic falls within the limits prescribed by 86.03 for the longest customary composite length of the vessel and its tow.

Subpart B-Bell or gong
§ 86.21 Intensity of signal.

A bell or gong, or other device having similar sound characteristics shall produce a sound pressure level of not less than 110 dB at 1 meter.

§ 86.23 Construction.

Bells and gongs shall be made of corrosion-resistant material and designed to give a clear tone. The diameter of the mouth of the bell shall be not less than 300 mm for vessels of more than 20 meters in length, and shall be not less than 200 mm for vessels of 12 to 20 meters in length. The mass of the striker shall be not less than 3 percent of the mass of the bell. The striker shall be capable of manual operation.

NOTE: When practicable, a power-driven bell striker is recommended to ensure constant force.

Subpart C-Approval

§ 86.31 Approval. (Reserved)

INLAND

ANNEX IV

DISTRESS SIGNALS

§ 87.1 Need of assistance.

The following signals, used or exhibited either together or separately, indicate distress and need of assistance:

a) A gun or other explosive signal fired at intervals of about a minute;

b) A continuous sounding with any fog-signalling apparatus;

c) Rockets or shells, throwing red stars fired one at a time at short intervals;

d) A signal made by radiotelegraphy or by any other signaling method consisting of the group ··· ___ ··· (SOS) in the Morse Code;

e) A appropriate signal transmitted by radiotelephony consisting of the spoken word "Mayday";

f) The International Code Signal of distress indicated by N.C.;

g) A signal consisting of a square flag having above or below it a ball or anything resembling a ball;

h) Flames on the vessel (as from a burning tar barrel, oil barrel, etc.);

i) A rocket parachute flare or a hand flare showing a red light;

j) A smoke signal giving off orange-colored smoke;

k) Slowly and repeatedly raising and lowering arms outstretched to each side;

l) The radiotelegraph alarm signal;

m) The radiotelephone alarm signal;

n) Signals transmitted by emergency position-indicating radio beacons;

o) A high intensity white light flashing at regular intervals from 50-70 times per minute.

§ 87.3 Exclusive use.
The use or exhibition of any of the foregoing signals except for the purpose of indicating distress and need of assistance and the use of other signals which may be confused with any of the above signals is prohibited.

§ 87.5 Supplemental signals.
Attention is drawn to the relevant sections of the International Code of Signals, the Merchant Ship Search and Rescue Manual and the following signal:

(a) a piece of orange-colored canvas with either a black square and circle or other appropriate symbol (for identification from the air);

(b) a dye marker.

ANNEX V

PILOT RULES

§ 88.01 Purpose and applicability.
This Part applies to all vessels operating on United States inland waters and to United States vessels operating on the Canadian waters of the Great Lakes to the extent there is no conflict with Canadian law.

§ 88.03 Definitions.
The terms used in this part have the same meaning as defined in the Inland Navigation Rules Act of 1980.

§ 88.05 Copy of rules.
After January 1, 1983, the operator of each self-propelled vessel 12 meters or more in length shall carry on board and maintain for ready reference a copy of the Inland Navigation Rules.

§ 88.09 Temporary exemption from light and shape requirements when operating under bridges.
A vessel's navigation lights and shapes may be lowered if necessary to pass under a bridge.

§ 88.11 Law enforcement vessels.
(a) Law enforcement vessels may display a flashing blue light when engaged in direct law enforcement activities. This light shall be located so that it does not interfere with the visibility of the vessel's navigation lights.
(b) The blue light described in this section may be displayed by law enforcement vessels of the United States and the States and their political subdivisions.

§ 88.13 Lights on barges at bank or dock.
(a) The following barges shall display at night and, if practicable, in periods of restricted visibility the lights described in paragraph (b) of this section-
(1) Every barge projecting into a buoyed or restricted channel.

(2) Every barge so moored that it reduces the available navigable width of any channel to less than 80 meters.

(3) Barges moored in groups more than two barges wide or to a maximum width of over 25 meters.

(4) Every barge not moored parallel to the bank or dock.

(b) Barges described in paragraph (a) shall carry two unobstructed white lights of an intensity to be visible for at least one mile on a clear dark night, and arranged as follows:

(1) On a single moored barge, lights shall be placed on the two corners farthest from the bank or dock.

(2) On barges moored in group formation, a light shall be placed on each of the upstream and downstream ends of the group, on the corners farthest from the bank or dock.

(3) Any barge in a group, projecting from the main body of the group toward the channel, shall be lighted as a single barge.

(c) Barges moored in any slip or slough which is used primarily for mooring purposes are exempt from the lighting requirements of this section.

(d) Barges moored in well-illuminated areas are exempt from the lighting requirements of this section. These areas are as follows:

Chicago Sanitary Ship Canal

(1) Mile 293.2 to 293.9
(3) Mile 295.2 to 296.1
(5) Mile 297.5 to 297.8
(7) Mile 298 to 298.2
(9) Mile 298.6 to 298.8
(11) Mile 299.3 to 299.4
(13) Mile 299.8 to 300.5
(15) Mile 303 to 303.2
(17) Mile 303.7 to 303.9
(19) Mile 305.7 to 305.8
(21) Mile 310.7 to 310.9
(23) Mile 311 to 311.2

(25) Mile 312.5 to 312.6
(27) Mile 313.8 to 314.2
(29) Mile 314.6
(31) Mile 314.8 to 315.3
(33) Mile 315.7 to 316
(35) Mile 316.8
(37) Mile 316.85 to 317.05
(39) Mile 317.5
(41) Mile 318.4 to 318.9
(43) Mile 318.7 to 318.8
(45) Mile 320 to 320.3
(47) Mile 320.6
(49) Mile 322.3 to 322.4
(51) Mile 322.8
(53) Mile 322.9 to 327.2

Calumet Sag Channel
(61) Mile 316.5

Little Calumet River
(71) Mile 321.2
(73) Mile 322.3

Calumet River
(81) Mile 328.5 to 328.7
(83) Mile 329.2 to 329.4
(85) Mile 330, west bank to 330.2

(87) Mile 331.4 to 331.6
(89) Mile 332.2 to 332.4
(91) Mile 332.6 to 332.8

Cumberland River
(101) Mile 126.8
(103) Mile 191

§ 88.15 Lights on dredge pipelines.

Dredge pipelines that are floating or supported on trestles shall display the following lights at night and in periods of restricted visibility.

(a) One row of yellow lights. The lights must be-

(1) Flashing 50-70 times per minute,

(2) Visible all around the horizon,

(3) Visible for at least 2 miles on a clear dark night,

(4) Not less than 1 and not more than 3.5 meters above the water,

(5) Approximately equally spaced, and

(6) Not more than 10 meters apart where the pipeline crosses a navigable channel. Where the pipeline does not cross a navigable channel the lights must be sufficient in number to clearly show the pipeline's length and course.

(b) Two red lights at each end of the pipeline, including the ends in a channel where the pipeline is separated to allow vessels to pass (whether open or closed). The lights must be-

(1) Visible all around the horizon, and

(2) Visible for at least 2 miles on a clear dark night, and

(3) One meter apart in a vertical line with the lower light at the same height above the water as the flashing yellow light.

PENALTY PROVISIONS VIOLATIONS OF INTERNATIONAL NAVIGATION RULES AND REGULATIONS (33 U.S.C. 1608)

Sec. 9.(a) Whoever operates a vessel, subject to the provisions of this Act, in violation of this Act or of any regulation promulgated pursuant to section 8, shall be liable to a civil penalty of not more than $5,000 for each violation.

(b) Every vessel subject to the provisions of this Act, other than a public vessel being used for noncommercial purposes, which is operated in violation of this Act or of any regulation promulgated pursuant to section 8, shall be liable to a civil penalty of not more than $5,000 for each such violation, for which penalty the vessel may be seized and proceeded against in the district court of the United States of any district within which such vessel may be found.

(c) The Secretary of the department in which the Coast Guard is operating may assess any civil penalty authorized by this section. No such penalty may be assessed until the person charged, or the owner of the vessel charged, as appropriate, shall have been given notice of the violation involved and an opportunity for a hearing. For good cause shown, the Secretary may remit, mitigate, or compromise any penalty assessed. Upon the failure of the person charged, or the owner of the vessel charged, to pay an assessed penalty, as it may have been mitigated or compromised, the Secretary may request the Attorney General to commence an action in the appropriate district court of the United States for collection of the penalty as assessed, without regard to the amount involved, together with such other relief as may be appropriate. (July 27, 1977, § 9, 91, Stat 310)

VIOLATIONS OF INLAND NAVIGATION RULES AND REGULATIONS (33 U.S.C. 2072)

SEC. 4.(a) Whoever operates a vessel in violation of this Act, or of any regulation issued thereunder, or in violation of a certificate of alternative compliance issued under Rule 1 is liable to a civil penalty of not more than $5,000 for each violation.

(b) Every vessel subject to this Act, other than a public vessel being used for noncommercial purposes, that is operated in violation of this Act, or of any regulation issued thereunder, or in violation of a certificate of alternative compliance issued under Rule 1 is liable to a civil penalty of not more than $5,000 for each violation, for which penalty the vessel may be seized and proceeded against in the district court of the United States of any district within which the vessel may be found.

(c) The Secretary may assess any civil penalty authorized by this section. No such penalty may be assessed until the person charged, or the owner of the vessel charged, as appropriate, shall have been given notice of the violation involved and an opportunity for a hearing. For good cause shown, the Secretary may remit, mitigate, or compromise any penalty assessed. Upon the failure of the person charged, or the owner of the vessel charged, to pay an assessed penalty, as it may have been mitigated or compromised, the Secretary may request the Attorney General to commence an action in the appropriate district court of the United States for collection of the penalty as assessed, without regard to the amount involved, together with such other relief as may be appropriate.

(d) The Secretary of the Treasury shall withhold or revoke, at the request of the Secretary, the clearance, required by section 4197 of the Revised Statutes of the United States (46 U.S.C. 91) of any vessel, the owner or operator of which is subject to any of the penalties in this section. Clearance may be granted in such cases upon the filing of a bond or other surety satisfactory to the Secretary. (Dec. 24, 1980, § 4, 94 Stat. 3433)

DUTY OF MASTER OF VESSEL IN COLLISION TO GIVE AID, NAME OF HIS VESSEL, ETC. (33 U.S.C. 367)

In every case of collision between two vessels it shall be the duty of the master or person in charge of each vessel, if and so far as he can do so without serious danger to his own vessel, crew, and passengers (if any), to stay by the other vessel until he has ascertained that she has no need of further assistance, and to render to the other vessel, her master, crew, and passengers (if any) such assistance as may be practicable and as may be necessary in order to save them from any danger caused by the collision, and also to give to the master or person in charge of the other vessel the name of his own vessel and her port of registry, or the port or place to which she belongs, and also the name of the ports and places from which and to which she is bound. If he fails so to do, and no reasonable cause for such failure is shown, the collision shall, in the absence of proof to the contrary, be deemed to have been caused by his wrongful act, neglect, or default. (Sept. 4, 1890, c. 875, § 1, 26 Stat. 425)

PENALTY FOR FAILURE TO GIVE AID, ETC. (33 U.S.C. 368)

Every master or person in charge of a United States vessel who fails, without reasonable cause, to render such assistance or give such information as required in section 367 of this title shall be deemed guilty of a misdemeanor, and shall be liable to a penalty of $1,000, or imprisonment for a term not exceeding two years; and for the above sum the vessel shall be liable and may be seized and proceeded against by process in any district court of the United States by any person; one-half such sum to be payable to the informer and the other half to the United States. (Sept. 4, 1890, c. 875, § 2, 26 Stat. 425)

NEGLIGENT OPERATION: RENDERING OF ASSISTANCE IN CASUALTIES: PENALTIES (46 U.S.C. 1453 et seq.; 85 Stat 215) EXCERPTS FROM THE FEDERAL BOAT SAFETY ACT OF 1971

Applicability

Sec. 4.(a) This Act applies to vessels and associated equipment used, to be used, or carried in vessels used, on waters subject to the jurisdiction of the United States and on the high seas beyond the territorial seas for vessels owned in the United States.

* * *

(c) This Act, except those sections where the content expressly indicates otherwise, does not apply to-

(1) foreign vessels temporarily using waters subject to United States jurisdiction;

(2) military or public vessels of the United States, except recreational-type public vessels;

(3) a vessel whose owner is a State or subdivision thereof, which is used principally for governmental purposes, and which is clearly identifiable as such;

(4) ships' lifeboats.

* * * * *

Prohibited Acts

Sec. 12.(a)

* * *

(c) No person may use a vessel in violation of this Act or regulations issued thereunder.

(d) No person may use a vessel, including one otherwise exempted by section 4(c) of this Act, in a negligent manner so as to endanger the life, limb, or property of any person. Violations of this subsection involving use which is grossly negligent, subject the violator, in addition to any other penalties prescribed in this Act, to the criminal penalties prescribed in section 34.

* * * * *

Rendering of Assistance in Casualties

Sec. 16.(a) The operator of a vessel, including one otherwise exempted by subsection 4(c) of this Act, involved in a collision, accident, or other casualty, to the extent he can do so without serious danger to his own vessel, or persons aboard, shall render all practical and necessary assistance to persons affected by the collision, accident, or casualty to save them from danger caused by the collision, accident, or casualty. He shall also give his name, address, and the identification of his vessel to any person injured and to the owner of any property damaged. The duties imposed by this subsection are in addition to any duties otherwise imposed by law.

(b) Any person who complies with subsection (a) of this section or who gratuitously and in good faith renders assistance at the scene of a vessel collision, accident, or other casualty without objection of any person assisted, shall not be held liable for any civil damages as a result of the rendering of assistance or for any act or omission in providing or arranging salvage, towage, medical treatment, or other assistance where the assisting person acts as an ordinary, reasonably prudent man would have acted under the same or similar circumstances.

* * * *

Criminal Penalties

Sec. 34. Any person who willfully violates section 12(c) of this Act or the regulations issued thereunder shall be fined not more than $1,000 for each violation or imprisoned not more than one year, or both.

Civil Penalties

Sec. 35.(a) ***

(b) In addition to any other penalty prescribed by law any person who violates any other provision of this Act or the regulations issued thereunder shall be liable to a civil penalty of not more than $500 for each violation. If the violation involves the use of a vessel, the vessel, except as exempted by subsection 4(c) of this Act, shall be liable and may be proceeded against in the district court of any district in which the vessel may be found.

For Vessel Bridge-to-Bridge Radiotelephone Regulations and any test questions pertaining thereto see Code of Federal Regulations (CFR) 33 Part 26.

A

B

C

D

E

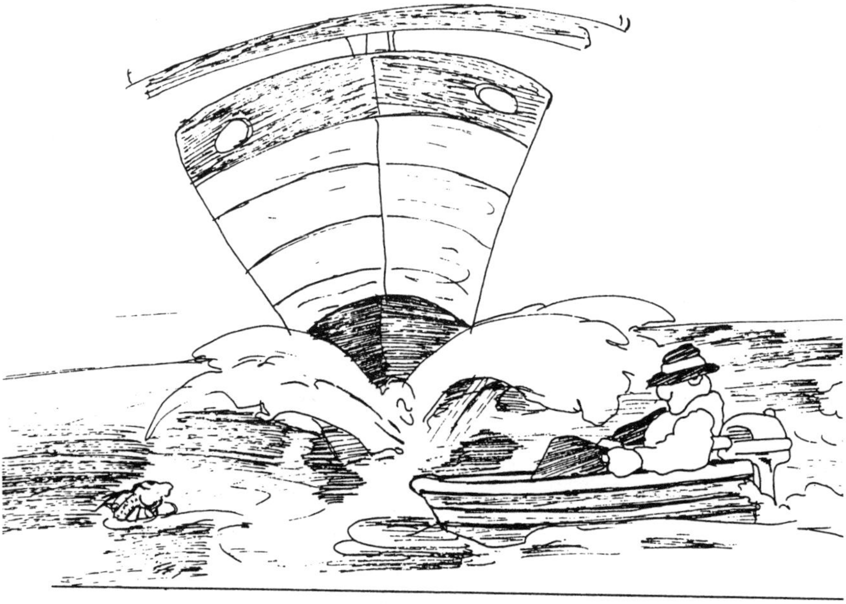

Sail has the right-of-way over power.

SEE PAGE 229 FOR VIDEO DESCRIPTIONS

The order form on the next page consists of items of considerable use to CG license candidates. Each is less than similar items available in most retail stores. This is a description and cost of each item. All are shipped on a one day turnaround basis.

1) The Coast Guard License - From Six Pac to Masters 100 tons - 13th Ed. This book is published about once each year with applicable updates. First published in 1972 the book has enjoyed an enduring tenure. Our files are resplendent with letters from those who acquired their license using only this book. $24.95

2) Please see page 224 for video descriptions and availability.

3) The Chartlets. Black and white *full size* quality facsimiles of the four charts currently in use in the REC's. 11462-Alligator Reef, 12221-Chesapeake, 12354-Long Is. Sound. 13205-Block Island. Each comes with CG quiz questions and answers. Better to become familiar with strange charts now than in the REC exam room when time is precious. $6.95 each, or $22.95 **for all four. Not to be used for on-board navigation.**

4) The Supplement-Over 800 **additional** quiz questions direct from CG data banks. Cheap reassurance before your big day at the REC. $12.95.

5) Gonder's Rules of The Road. A definitive work. Charters West production of the Official Rules of The Road - word-for-word plus **including the newly revised Rules effective 1990-91.** Facing pages with simplified interpretations constructed especially for CG license aspirants. Don't even **think** about sitting for your ticket without reading this manual. Contains **some** illustrations and graphics also found in CG License Book. $12.95.

6) Course Plotter. Thick, sturdy simple type hard to find. Shown in text. Measures about 4" x 15" for both small and standard chart work. $7.95.

7) Flashcards-uncut, nine to a page. Eighty-eight separate panels. Lights, dayshapes, fog signals and visibility of lights memory crutches. Cut, will fit in your pocket to carry anywhere for study during free time. Color coded and printed on 8 1/2" x 11" #67 cardstock ready to color if you like. Not a stack of inappropriate repeats like so many expensive glossy sets on the market. $7.95.

8) Dividers. Small, simple and compact with plastic case. $5.95.

9) A dozen charting problems similar to those found in the text. Written **and** charted solutions included. The Second Dirty Dozen. $3.95.

10) Updates and errata, if any. Shipped with all orders or **FREE** upon request if you send a self-addressed stamped envelope.

SHIPPING COSTS FOR PAGE 230

All orders are shipped United Parcel Service so please -no P.O. boxes if avoidable.

Forty-Eight States

Orders less than $20, shipping cost is $2.00. If more, add $3.50

Hawaii/Alaska

All orders are shipped U.S. Postage or UPS 2nd Day Air. **Your choice.**

U.S. Postage-if order is less than $20, add $2.50. If $20 or more add $3.50

All UPS shipments are 2nd Day air. Add $6.50 for orders less than $20; $8.50 for $20 or more.

VIDEOS BY CHARTERS WEST

HIGH RESOLUTION QUALITY TAPES PRODUCED IN OUR OWN STUDIOS

1) **THE COAST GUARD LICENSE - From Six Pac to Master 100 Tons.**
License application and sea time tips. An overview with definitions of the four categories (modules) for Six Pac to Master 100 tons. An informal, but precise video defining the parameters and requirements for the license. Discussion on the Codes of Federal Regulations (CFR's) and how they are to be used in the open book exams in the REC's. Which books carry what information. Discussions on *Light List* and *Coast Pilot* and what to expect and look for in prepping for the exam. Tips on the piloting quiz and a full size display of the four charts used in the REC and how to acquire them cheaply. Now available $19.95

2) **RULES OF THE ROAD - All Coast Guard Licenses and Renewals**
Heavy on informal animation. Good for all candidates from Six Pac to Master Unlimited Tonnage and Oceans. Lights and dayshapes. Arcs of visibility. Maneuvering signals with appropriate whistle signals. Maneuvering and signals in restricted visibility, at anchor and aground. A clear animated definition of the elusive pecking order-the various rights-of-way of all vessels afloat. Run it again and again until you have it straight. Heavy on Rules specifics and quiz tips. Now available - $19.95.

3) **PILOTING - As Required For Coast Guard License Candidates.**
Navigation for the Six Pac up to and including Master 100 Tons. Step-by-step hands-on procedure assuming no one knows anything. Follow along. Slow and easy. From simplifying variation and deviation to computations on speed-distance-time, course plotter how-to, dead reckoning, running fixes, bearings and set and drift. Not just a face talking at you. This tape was made with a mind to teaching offshore piloting to chimpanzees. Author Budd Gonder's methodical and humorous approach utilizing the white board as a simulated chart. Like our other tapes, run it again and again until you have it straight. How to learn and love it at the same time. Available by winter 1990. $19.95.

4) **THE U.S. BUOYAGE SYSTEM - A Indispensable Necessity For Any License.**
Animated with super-accurately reproduced models. A new approach to an old adversary of every candidate. Includes all four systems: The oceans lateral system, the Rivers, the Intracoastal Waterways (ICW) and the Uniform State Buoyage system. Knowledge of all four is required for any coastal license. Includes the buoy light signals, meanings and definitions of all systems. Make your study life easier. Available late Spring, 1991. $19.95

CHARTERS WEST ORDER FORM 5-RR

☏ 1-800-SEA-TEST (1-800-732-8378)-FOR ORDERS ONLY* ☏
FOR SUPPORT - CALL (805) 565-1050

VISA & M/C ONLY-PLEASE- NO CHARGE ORDERS FOR LESS THAN $10.

PLEASE READ PAGES 228-229 BEFORE ORDERING

1) The Coast Guard License Book — $24.95-$________
   Six Pac to Masters - 100 tons.

2) The VHS Videos - Read page 229 before ordering videos.
   - The Coast Guard License — $19.95-$________
   - Rules of The Road — $19.95-$________
   - Piloting-For Coast Guard Exams — Available Winter 1990 — $19.95-$________
   - The U.S. Buoyage System — Available Spring-1991 — $19.95-$________

3) The Chartlets. Circle those desired. 11462, 12221, 12354, 13205. See page 228 for number ID. $6.95 ea. or $22.95 for complete set. Includes plotting questions from CG data banks for each separate chart. — -$________

4) The Supplement. Over 800 additional quiz questions in all modules. — $12.95-$________

5) Gonder's Rules of The Road — $12.95-$________
   With illustrated version in English.

6) Course Plotter. No frills. — $7.95-$________
   Similar to one in text. Sturdy-accurate.

7) Flashcards-Uncut to save $$ - on 8 1/2" x 11" cardstock. — $7.95-$________

8) Dividers. For measuring distances & plotting latitude and longitude on charts. With plastic envelope. — $5.95-$________

9) The Second Dirty Dozen-Charting problems with detailed answers and chart solutions as in Coast Guard Lic. text. — $3.95-$________

California Residents
must add applicable sales tax for your district & county — $________

For all shipping costs and specials to Alaska/Hawaii/Puerto Rico please see page 228. Total Shipping — $________

TOTAL-$________

PLEASE RUSH THIS ORDER TO:

Name________________________________

Street-(No P.O. Boxes for UPS)________________________________

City____________________State____________Zip______

Mail your order to Charters West-P.O. Box 597 - Summerland, CA 93067

***PHONE ORDERS - MASTERCHARGE OR VISA ONLY - 1-800-SEA-TEST - IF A RECORDING CUTS IN PLEASE LEAVE YOUR NAME AND PHONE NUMBER - WE'LL GET BACK TO YOU.**

Prices subject to change without notice, but probably won't.